In order to embrace your inner Wabi Sabi first you must understand what
confuse it with wasabi, that is the tubes of green hot sauce you squeeze c

There is no literal translation for the term Wabi Sabi into English from the
were not originally attached together and their meanings have changed ove ...s.

Wabi is said to have traditionally have meant living away from society; being desolate and alone; living in harmony with nature. Peace, tranquillity and balance. This also lends itself towards translation as rustic simplicity, unostentatiousness, a gentle affection for the antique. It has evolved to mean simplicity, freshness and rustic beauty therefore bringing it closer the translation of Sabi.

Sabi has developed from its more simple meaning of growing old or to be desolate and now refers to a beauty that comes from weathering and age, an understanding of the cycles of life, the need for mending and the idea that objects become more beautiful and valuable through this process.

Joined together the two blend to create a theory that spans all aspects of life, from design to everyday living. It is actually very complex and could take a lifetime to fully understand. However, it is not bound by a complex set of rules like Feng Shui. This is not about learning a new way of living or radically altering the way you are, but understanding how life works and how you can become more comfortable with it so you can enjoy it more.

The key points of Wabi Sabi are that everything is:

Imperfect Impermanent Incomplete

However, if I was to summarise Wabi Sabi in three easier to use everyday words I would say:

Authentic, Relaxed and Ongoing

It does not quite cover the full theory but it gives you the general idea. It is a way of helping you look at the Wabi Sabi concept so it can be applied to your life today in an uncomplicated manner.

And if you asked Mary Poppins to explain she would most likely say:

“How to be perfectly imperfect in every way”.

Right now this may not mean much to you but as the book progresses all become clear, however in essence you should be starting realise we are not expecting perfection here....

Appreciation of natural objects and processes

Nature surrounds us every day. The easiest thing to define is the objects in our environment that we can see such as trees, plants, rocks, soil and other non-man-made items. We are born with an appreciation for beauty and all have a landscape that we prefer be it the mountains, desert or the sea. Over the centuries Artists have been drawn to study the landscape around us in great depth, the changing seasons, the effect that varying light has on the same field or haystack. They sought to capture the details and textures in even the simplest everyday objects.

Natural processes, however, are less obvious. Growth is a natural process and in reverse so are erosion and decay. Waterflow, fire, transfer of colour from plants/earth, drying out, warming up, freezing and more. The biggest natural process, of course, is life itself.

Craftspeople have used natural processes within their practice for centuries. They have an element of randomness within them and just as we cannot control the wind or tame the sea, we cannot fully control these methods within our practice. For instance the moment we place the paintbrush upon the surface of the page the water and the pigment start to move and as trained as we are we cannot completely influence it's movement. We can study for years to work with it and develop a style that manipulates it we will always be at the mercy of nature.

Many artists use this element of chance as part of their practice embracing the imperfections and process of creation where they are the catalyst that then lets nature finish the job. Raku firing for instance is an excellent example of potters making a piece, glazing it and then being at the mercy of the flames for the final aspect of the firing process. Many pots are broken but the results are so beautiful it is worth the risk.

For many of us the idea of letting go of control is difficult. Inside us all is a little bit of a control freak. For some of us it is small and for others it is much, much larger (you know where you fit). The idea of using a process that relinquishes an element of control and embraces the concept of randomness for many would be way beyond the comfort zone. However, life pushes us beyond that comfort zone and reminds us that we cannot be in control, and maybe do not need to be, more and more often as we get older.

Let me explain one way that I learnt to let go a little of the (rather large) control freak inside me. I have four children (yes four), when my first child was born I followed him everywhere checking him every few minutes to make sure he was still breathing, hovered around him helping him do everything and followed all the rules as I was told to. Child number two came along four years later and by then I felt I could give him a little more space, I followed him from six feet away rather than one. I checked him each hour instead of every ten minutes while he slept and I broke a couple of rules! By child number three another four years later I was happy to be in the other room and know he was still alive and breathing and when child number four came along yet another four years down the line, well, she looks after me!

All four children are healthy, happy and independent regardless of my differing parenting styles, yet my stress levels were very different. This lead me to think that if my children could cope with being well adjusted and independent without me constantly hovering over them then maybe I could apply this to other aspects of my life. So, I took this into my workplace too and as a manager started to delegate more to my co-workers rather than take all the workload myself. I set deadlines for students and put the ball back in their court when they missed them rather than rearranging things because they had not done the work. It allowed me a whole different type of control rather than the constant whirlwind of the control freak I had been living in before.

Once you have found a way to release the inner control freak in you life will become that little bit easier and you can start to find your new type of control. You can enjoy the finer moments in life where you understand that there is nothing you can do about the right now and you will find a new appreciation for what you create and how you make it.

Remember, at no point did I say this was going to be easy (sorry), but I do promise it will work..

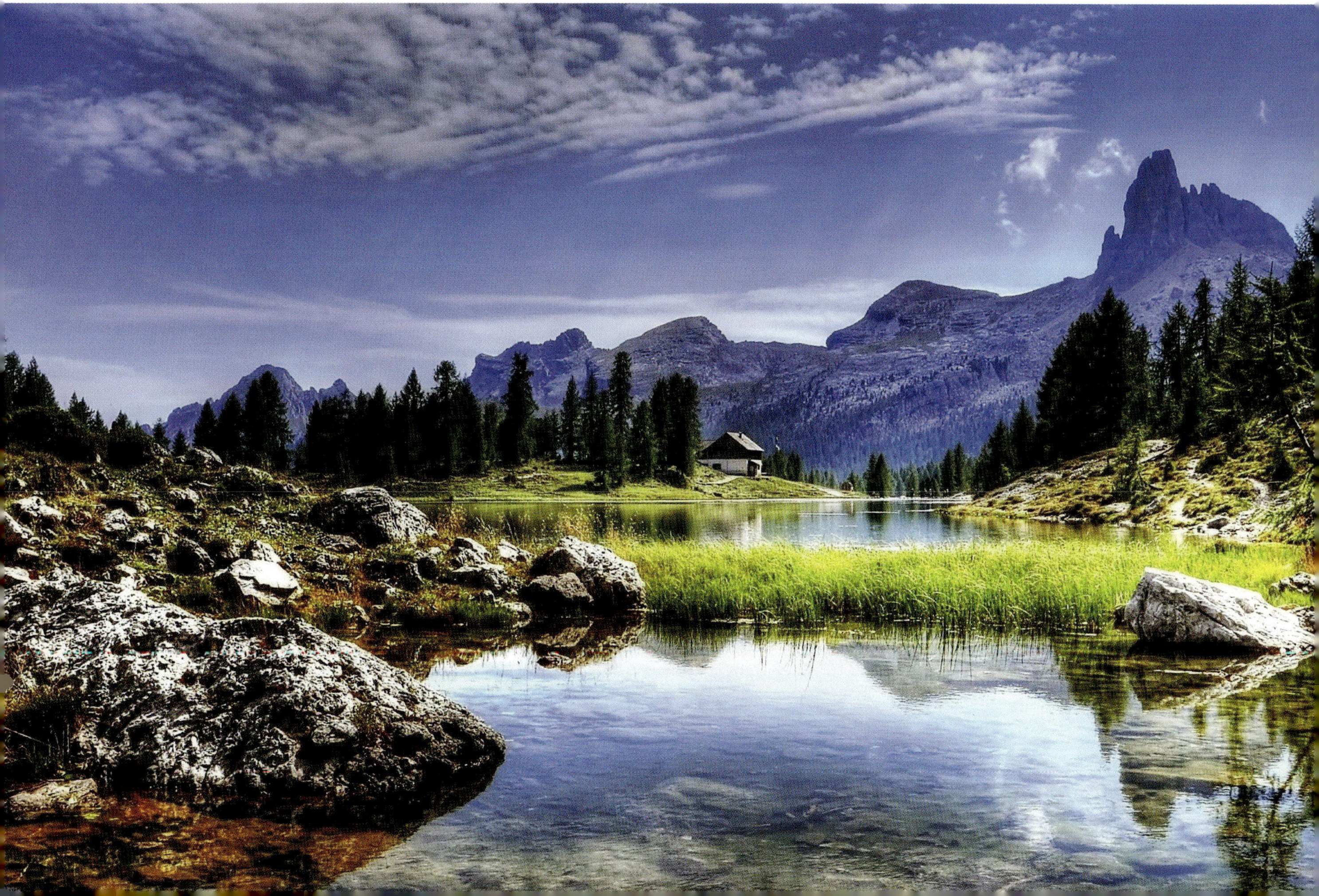

Project - Rust/Eco Dyeing

Rust and Eco dyeing is a natural process and one where you have to embrace your Wabi Sabi from the start. Control is limited to very few factors, your choice of material, your choice of objects/plants and then your layout. As you do more dyeing you will learn what combinations will create what colourways and have a greater degree of understanding about the results you will produce. With rust alone this is more predictable however, when you combine plants your location and the time of year will affect the outcome.

[Wear gloves at all times when working with rusty metal as it is bad for you!]

Soak and then lay out your plain fabric, natural fabrics work best especially if you are getting plants involved. You will not be able to use plants on their own without a mordant (way of getting the colour to stay in the fabric) but the rust does this for you.

Now place your rusty items on top. If you want to include plants this is the point to add them too - try anything, if it does not work you can always dye it again! Then lay another pre-soaked lighter weight fabric on top of this layer. This helps to stop too much transfer of colour into the wrong bits of the fabric when you roll and also makes two pieces of fabric at once!

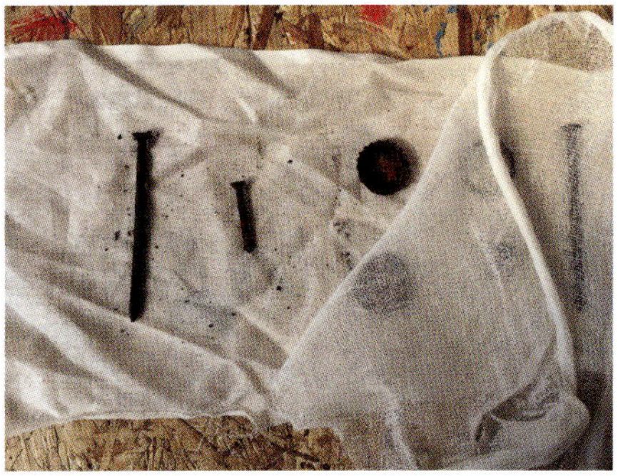

Now you can choose your natural reagent - depending on what you choose will affect the colour result. Either:

1) Vinegar/Salt Water. Both of these have similar results but the vinegar is faster. However it is pungent!

2) Tea/Coffee. Both of these have similar results but try them both as they will have differing effects on the background fabric and the rust. Also try different brands and types.

3) Mix and match. See what happens when you combine more than one natural reagent together.

Spray or pour some of your choice of 1,2 or 3 on to your prepared fabric and dye objects. You do not need to saturate the whole cloth just wet around and on the rusty items/plants. Then roll the fabric up as tight as you can with the items inside. The idea is to keep as much contact as possible between the rusty objects/plants and the fabric as you can. Next tie some string or thread around the bundle to keep it rolled up. If you use natural thread or string it will be dyed too and you can use it in your work afterwards.

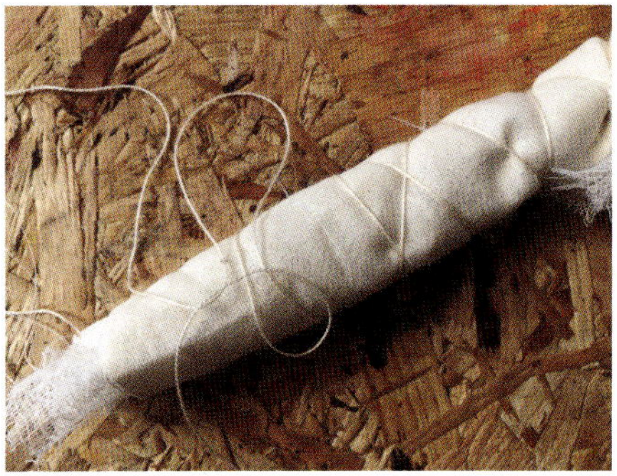

Leave your bundle for at least a week so the bundle can dry. The tea and coffee react quicker so keep watch as the colours change. If it dries too fast re-wet it to keep the reaction going until you get the colour you want. This can take up to three weeks, maybe more depending on your choice of fabric and your colour preference.

Once your bundle is dry and the right colour carefully unwrap and remove your rusty items for using again. Wash your fabric with a little fabric detergent and line dry. Take care as small bits of metal may remain in the fabric. Use your fabric for what you like!

Keep a logbook of what colours you make with which dyestuffs and which fabrics produce which results too so you can reproduce your favourites.

Reagent used	Rust/Plants	Fabrics	Time	Colour result

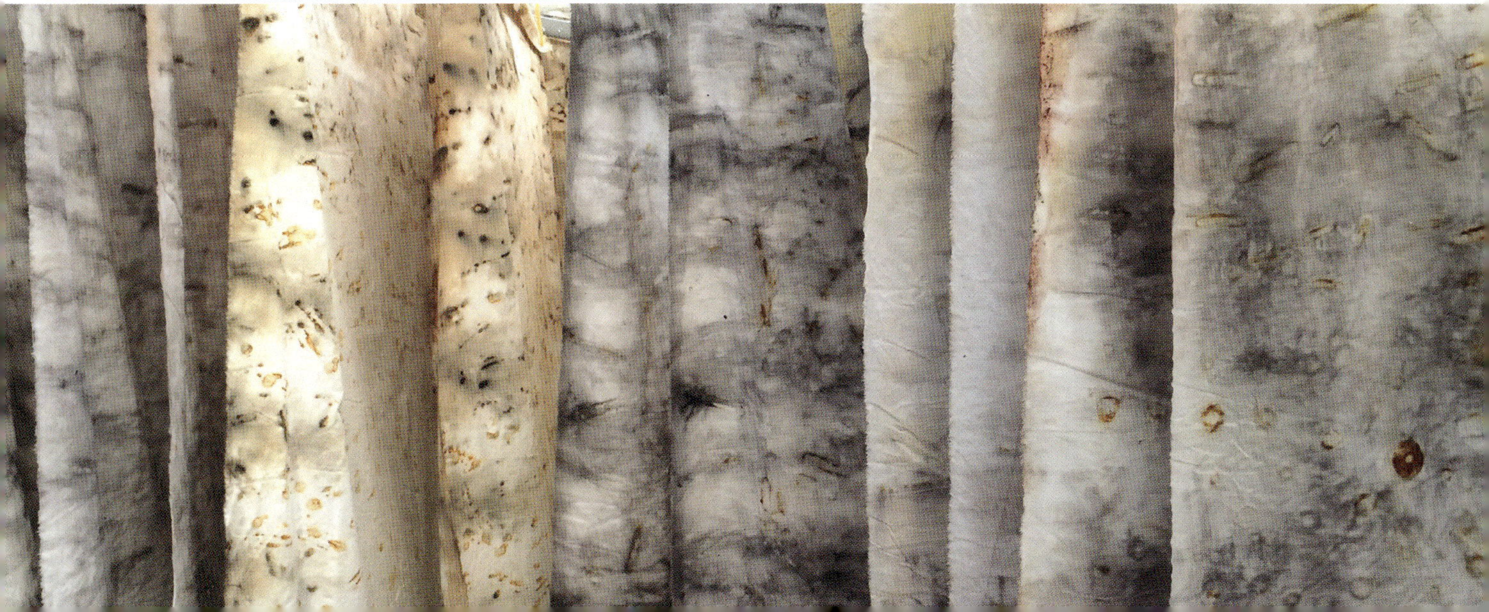

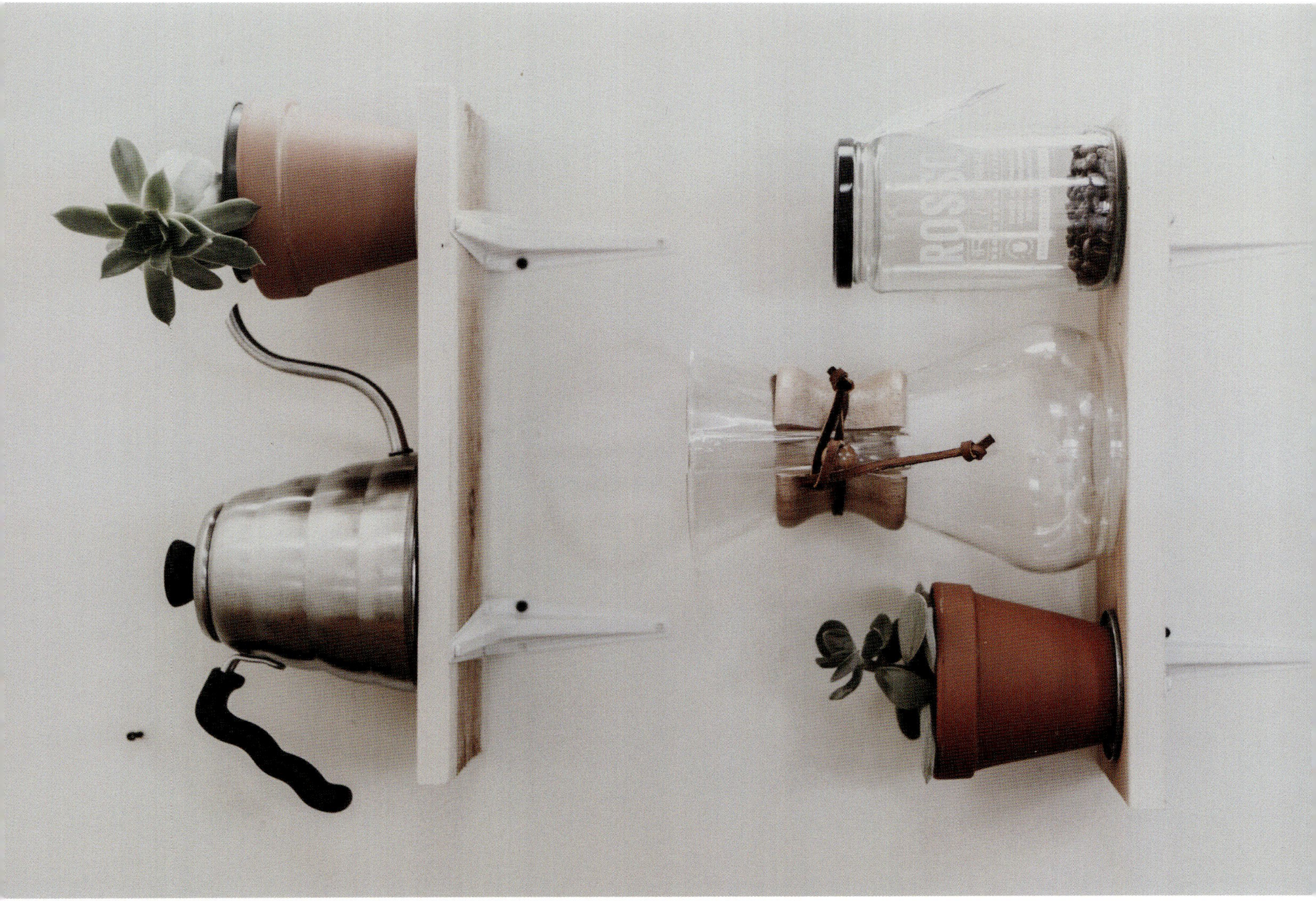

Wabi Sabi style - Chaotic balance. Nothing matches but there is a balance as your mind finds a way to create one in the correct arrangement of the objects. This also works when laying out fabric for a quilt or making a piece of Art. Our brain is adept at finding a way to make things 'work' without the need for a rigid pre-planned or symmetrical structure.

Asymmetry or Symmetry

Imagine you are given five pictures and asked to hang them on a wall. - Here is your wall, go ahead and hang them... (really, draw them on)

Look at you layout. Is it symmetrical, i.e. did you start with one in the middle and then put the others with the same pattern either side or did you get more freestyle and go for an asymmetrical layout where the two sides don't match?

This does not just have to be pictures, it can be any kind of arrangement like the plants in the picture to the left. There are five, an odd number, none of them match, and they have been placed in a manner that is not even across the shelves. This creates an asymmetrical balance - almost a chaotic harmony.

Nature is, more often than not, asymmetrical and as humans, on the whole, we prefer things in uneven numbers, 3,5,7 and so on. Subconsciously we need things to be in uneven numbers to feel more natural, for example, when designers are making virtual environments they are taught to place the scenery and plants in clusters of odd numbers so that they blend with the environment and they won't jump out at the player saying 'look at me I'm a group of plants'. When we arrange objects in our homes we often choose groupings of odd numbers even unintentionally.

Even we are not symmetrical. Have you ever taken a mirror and placed it on a photograph of your face to see how you would look if the two sides of your face were the same? It is fascinating to see what you would look like if your were perfectly symmetrical and what each side of your face makes you look like as they can be quite different. Research suggests that as a society we find people with more symmetrical faces more attractive. How symmetrical is your face and those in your family, and do you agree with this thought?

In the heyday of the Cinema, when actresses such as Elizabeth Taylor graced the Silver Screen, they knew which side of their face they preferred and when it came to their closeup they would know

Project - Felted Vessels

Wool is a natural fibre and when working with it you can never entirely predict the results meaning you have allow your inner Wabi Sabi to help you let go of some of the control. The shrinkage can vary depending on how far you work the fibres and what type if fibres you select. I have used merino for the orange vessel in my example as it is one of the more predictable fibres available.

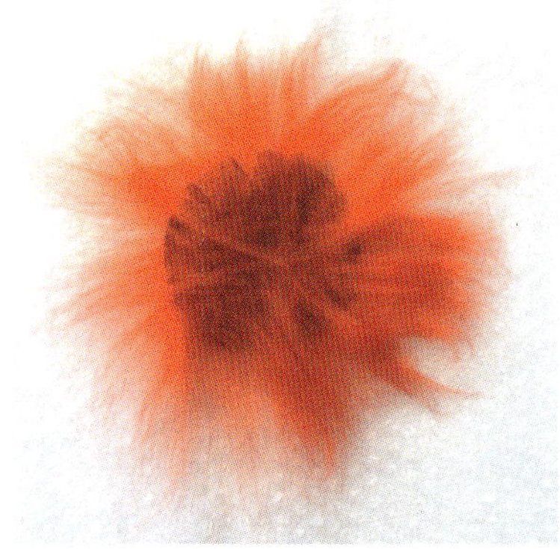

Lay a towel out on your work surface. This creates a base for your felting and keeps your work surface dry. On top of this place bubble wrap with the bubbles up.

Cut a circular plastic resist from something sturdy like pond liner or a very thick plastic sack, 10-15cm is a good starting diameter and as you progress you can play around with size. Place your circular plastic resist in the centre of the bubble wrap.

With dry hands take your main colour of wool tops. Hold it gently in one hand around the middle and put your other hand in the air as if you are about to high five someone, then bend from the middle of your hand. Use this motion to pull wisps of fibres from the bundles of tops. If you cannot pull then your hands are too close together. If the pieces are clumpy, tease them apart with your fingers to thin them out.

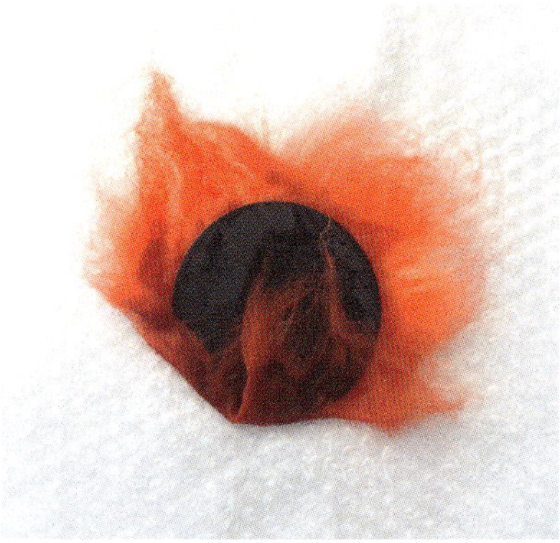

Start by placing your first layer down in a sunshine shape with the fibres half on and half off the circular resist. (top image) This layer needs to be thin enough to see through. Next place a second layer on top but only over the circle resist this time with the fibres running left to right. Keep it as thin as your first layer. Then place a third layer - this time with the fibres running top to bottom.

Using a jug or sprayer add some soapy water (a few squirts of liquid hand soap or washing up liquid in your water will do) to the centre of the fibres and fold in the bubble wrap. Press gently on the bubble wrap to spread the water through the fibres taking care not to fold the fibres over. Unfold the bubble wrap.

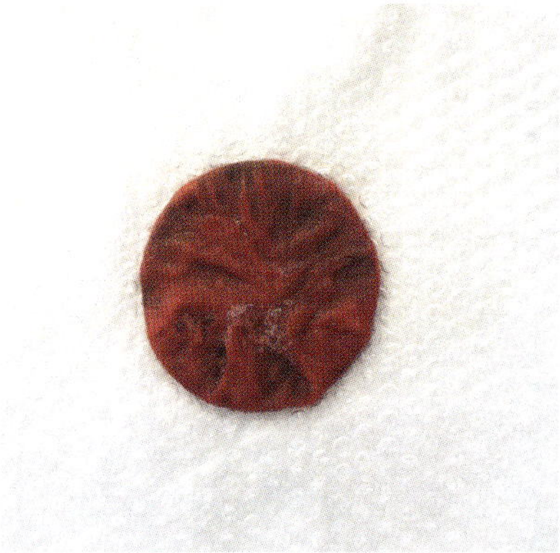

Now slide your finger underneath the fibres and the resist and pinch the two together then flip it over like a pancake. The resist is now on top of your fibres. Fold the fibres in to the middle of the resist (middle image) and smooth them gently from the edge to the middle so they are tight to avoid ridges when you felt. Once you have completely wrapped the fibres around the resist you are ready to go on to the next step. (bottom image previous page)

Repeat this process for a second time to thicken the vessel. The more times you repeat this process the less the vessel will shrink when felting. The minimum number of times you can do this is two with this size of resist which will use less wool fibres but your vessel will end up a lot smaller as it will shrink further. The maximum number of times you need to repeat this process with any size of resist is four however I have seen exceedingly thick vessels made from many more layers!

When placing down your final layer of wool you can add decorative fibres to it as this will be the top surface of your vessel. Look at the fibres, if you have any that are not pure wool make sure they are trapped underneath some of the wool fibres to make sure they felt in fully. Spread them out thinly however to add interest as they will shrink too when felted.

With each layer remember to wrap the fibres round well once you have flipped it over and use the bubble wrap to squeeze the water through to help the fibres stick together. Add more soapy water if you need to and don't rub just yet! Once you have all your layers placed and wrapped now you are ready to felt!

The science bit:

Felting is about getting the fibres to twist together around each other and shrink, different fibres do this more easily based on what length of 'crimp' they have. This is how much of a zigzag shape they have on their surface. To felt you need friction and moisture. Heat will speed up the process. The fastest way to felt is in the washing machine as it has all three (especially when you don't want to, think about the last time you made an accidental mini woolly jumper)

Fold your bubble wrap in half trapping the felting between the two layers. Use a carrier bag or more bubble wrap as a pad to rub the felt gently in circular motions working from the edge to the centre of the piece. (image to right) At this stage you do not want to move the fibres too much or you will undo your hard work of laying out. Rub gently on one side for 5 minutes then turn over and rub the other side for 5 minutes. You should see the fibres starting to look less fluffy.

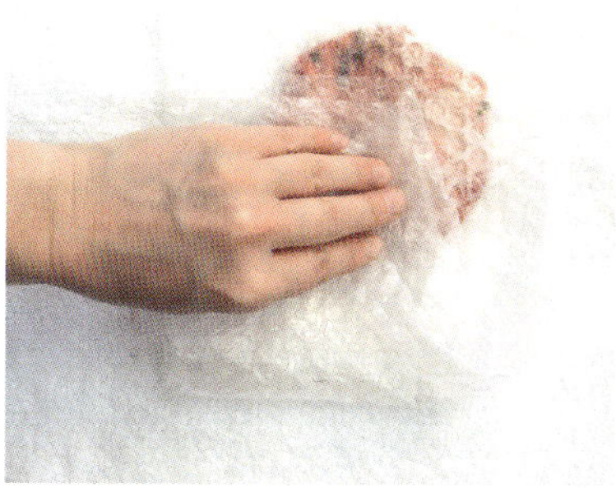

Once the fibres have started to felt you can use slightly more pressure so you can rub straight onto the surface of the felt with the bubble wrap, but still gently in circular motions. When the surface starts to feel like the fibres are not moving, test by pinching the surface gently and lifting to see how well they are holding together, you can go on to the next step.

Next, hold the felt in your hand and rub it onto the bubble wrap - this is more forceful and causes greater agitation to the fibres. Remember to work both sides of the felt. At this point the resist should start to feel like it is getting tight inside the felt. Now you need to open it up and take it out. Using a sharp pair of scissors make a small slit in the middle of one side through to the resist then pull the resist out. (top image) Keep the hole smaller than you want as it will stretch as you felt.

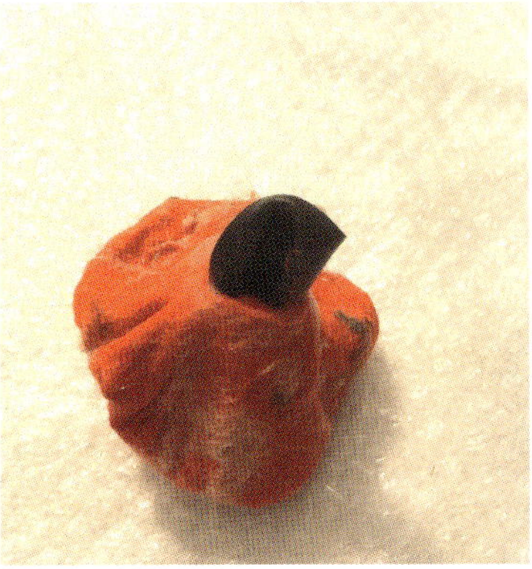

Using your finger and thumb rub the cut edges to felt them - this will make the hole more circular and smooth. Put your fingers inside and rub the vessel from inside and out using a combination of your fingers and the palm of your other hand. (middle image) This allows you to shape the vessel how you like. Push against the palm of your hand with your fingers to form the side walls of the vessel and shape your flat form into a 3D shape. Work round each section of the vessel until you are happy with the shape. Once it is complete wash it out in cold water and then reshape it with your hands stretching it back to the final shape you want and then leave it to dry.

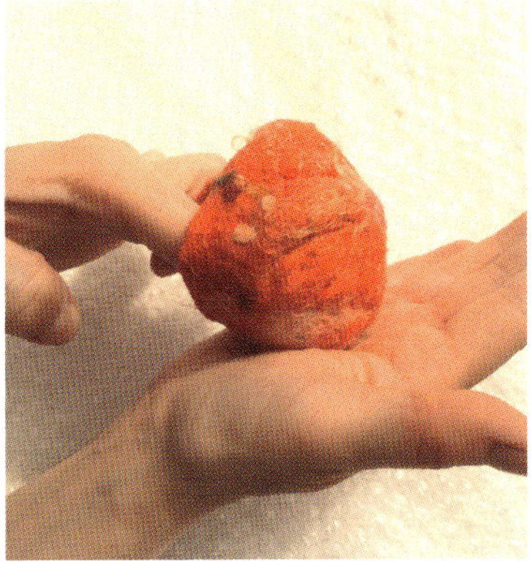

You can use your resist again as many times as you like so experiment with other ideas. Try larger or smaller resists, I have seen everything from a ring holder to a cat basket. You can also stitch into the felt once it is dry as the fabric produced is soft but solid.

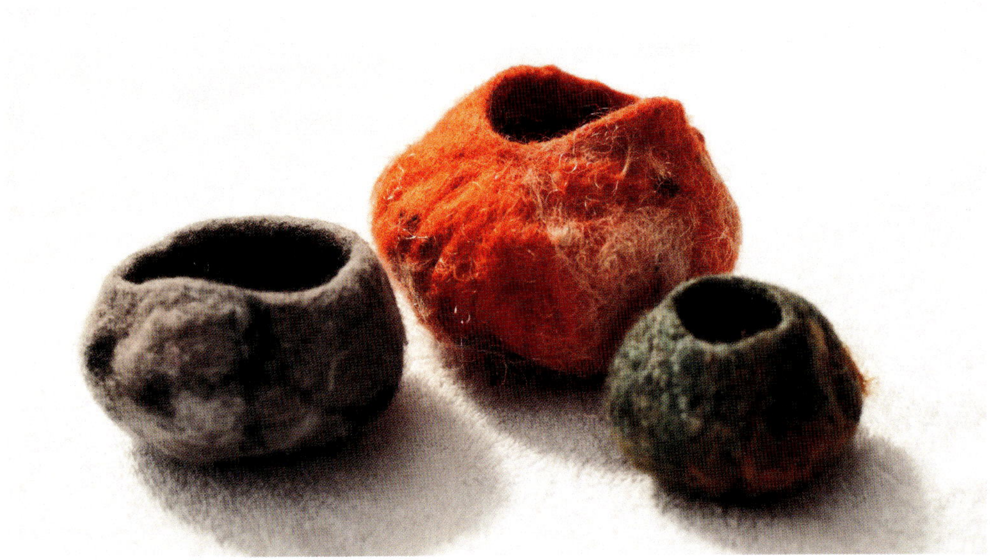

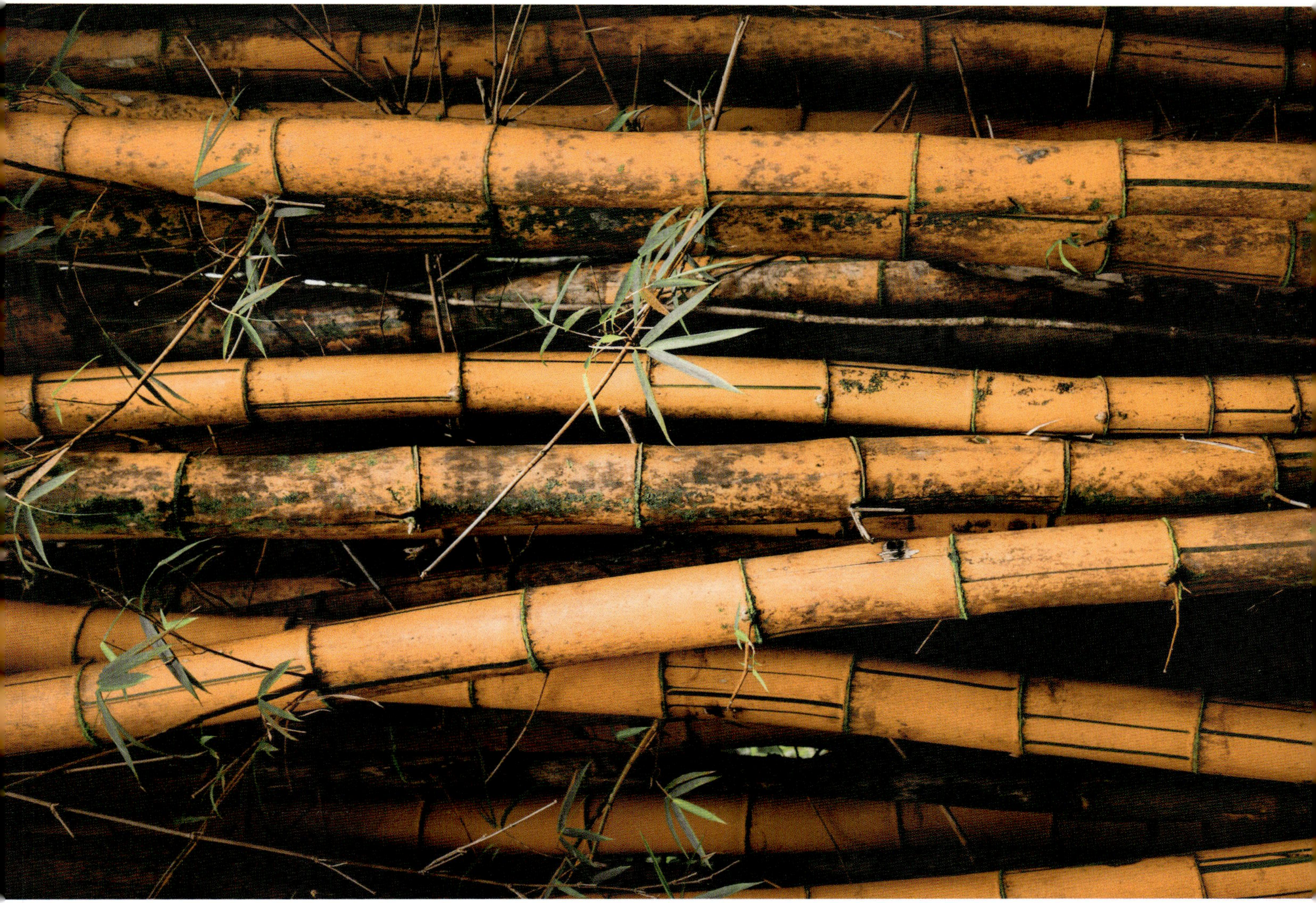

Wabi Sabi style - Drawing inspiration from natural forms. They are not perfect, the colours fluctuate and have surface blemishes, the shapes are irregular due to growth patterns. When replicating this therefore you need to make sure you are capturing these imperfections and irregularities.

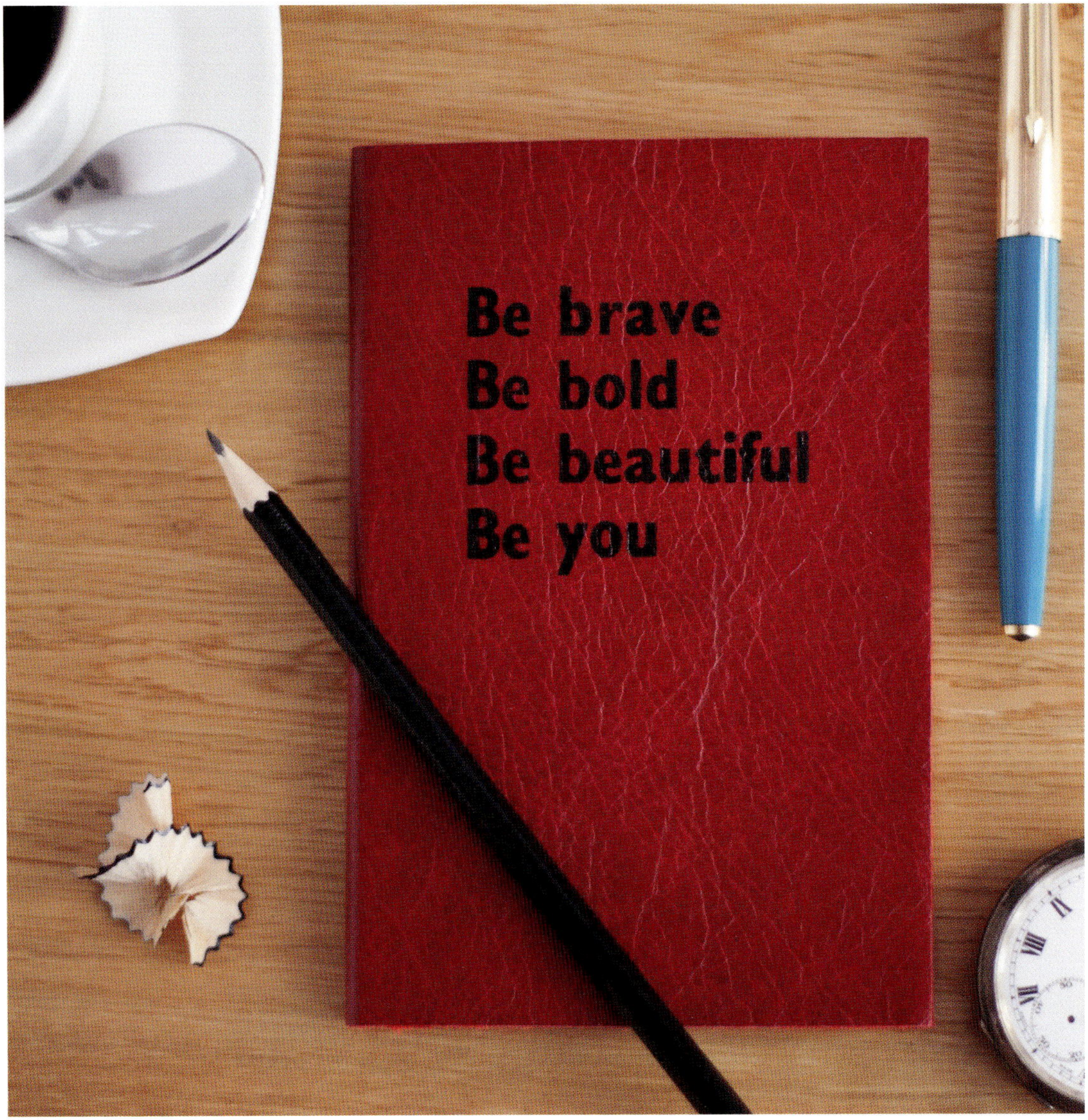
Be brave
Be bold
Be beautiful
Be you

which side they wanted to present to the camera; coining the phrase 'make sure you get my best side'.

Now, I know you are a selfie taker (I've seen your social media stream) and even though apparently after the age of 34 you shouldn't take selfies according to new research, hence my 2018 goal to get over my fear of doing so because I am definitely over the age of 34. When you are taking those selfies with your hand held high and the light just right, I bet you are making sure you are getting your best side in.

Interestingly I have always had a best side in my head and I gave in and asked my husband of 15 years the other day if he agreed and discovered he prefers the other side which gives support to what I am about to say.

Next time you are photographed or taking a selfie present your other cheek, your least favourite side, or go really radical and go full frontal (face of course!) because actually it's not one side or the other that makes you who you are, it's the whole face, in fact the whole of you. Because at the end of the day if someone as close to me as my husband thought the opposite to me what does the rest of the world think?

Highlighting imperfection not hiding it

When you got dressed this morning, be honest, did you put on an outfit to hide some part of your figure. Us ladies tend to be less fond of our hips, bums and bellies and crinkles (affectionate term for wrinkles in our house) and blokes it's normally and belly, crinkles or a loss of muscles tone thing as they get older.

Who are you hiding it from? What have you got to be ashamed of? When you walked out the door this morning looking radiant 99% of the people you walked past have never met the 10 years younger you that you spent the mirror time comparing yourself to as you got dressed. So you may not have walked out of the door looking like Naomi Campbell, but do you think Naomi Campbell walks out of the door looking like she does in the magazines every morning? No... and she does not look like 10 years younger her either! So give yourself a break and enjoy today as the you that you are now.

The biggest point that Wabi Sabi teaches us is that nothing in life is perfect. In fact that should be in bold so lets try again

NOTHING IN LIFE IS PERFECT

Our biggest problem with perfection as makers and humans is that we only see our mistakes. We scrutinise everything we do in such great detail that we focus in on the bits that don't work and

Project - Rethinking control

Step one

Think about all the things you tried to be in control of or got angry about recently that you actually had no ability to change. Fill in some of these things in the table below, I have put in one as an example to get you started. These things can be as big or as small as you like. They could be a one off occurrence or something that happens on a regular basis.

The traffic on the M6 motorway made me late

Step two

Next time you are faced with these things take a deep breath and say 'I can't control this so I won't let it make me angry' then think of what you will do instead for instance if you are stuck in traffic turn up the stereo and make the most of extra time to listen to your favourite music and say thank you for the chance to sing along or if the heel falls off your shoe instead of thinking 'aargh stupid shoes' think 'ooh I get to buy a new pair'.

Try doing this with the things you wrote on your list. What positives can you make from a seemingly negative situation?

I now know all the words to 'Sweet Home Alabama' at last.

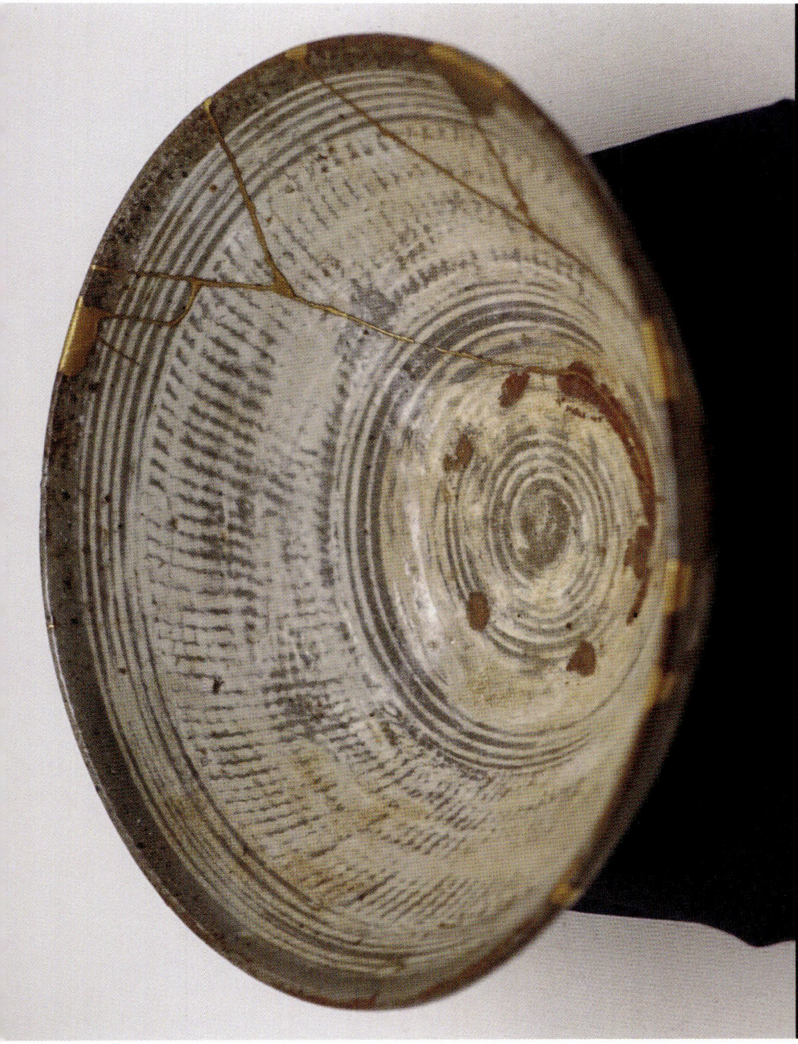

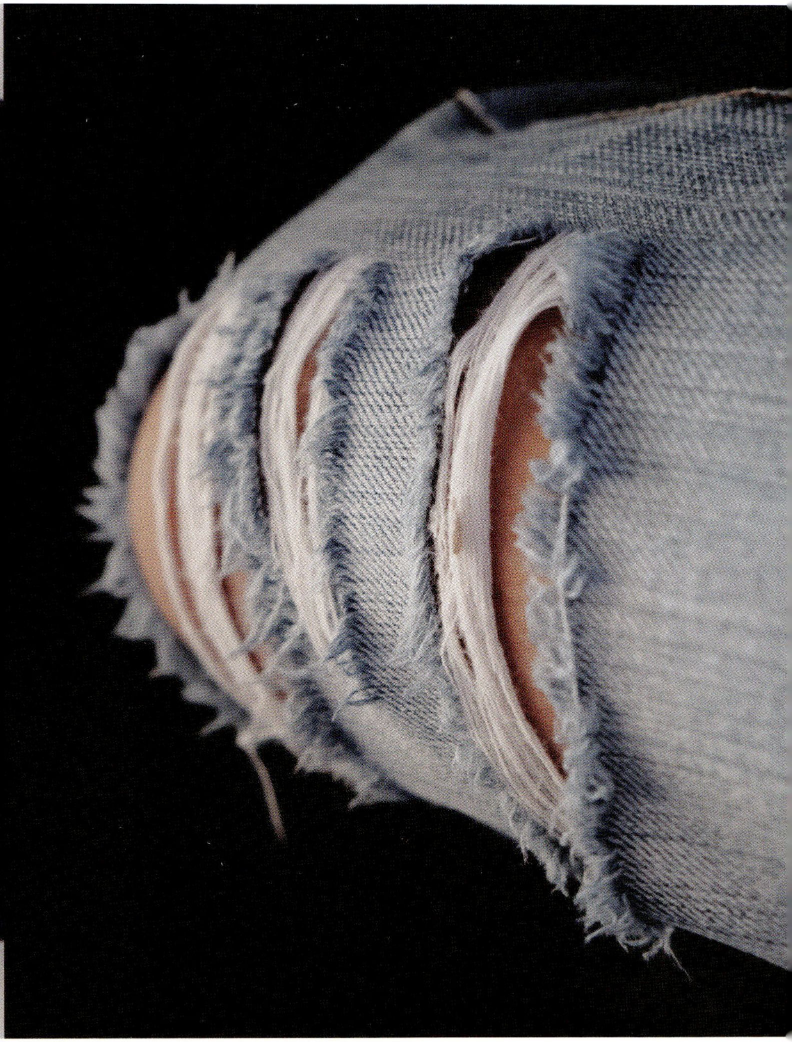

Wabi Sabi style - The art of mending and using not replacing is a core concept in Wabi Sabi style. It gives new life to objects and reminds us that we are not replaced when were are in need of repair. The item is more beautiful once it has been fixed and is often viewed as a new object now.

then, in an almost self-harming way, we like to announce them everyone who looks at it, eats it, visits it. However they interact with whatever it was we were doing, we declare loudly what went wrong. If we just let them see it with fresh eyes or eat it with an open mind they probably wouldn't know it was supposed to be duck a l'orange not lemon or that the apple tree was supposed to be two foot taller until you slipped with the chainsaw!

Artists and craftspeople are the worst for chastising themselves over imperfection. They can see every little mark that didn't go to plan and every stitch that skipped. The audience of course only sees the final product and appreciates it as a whole not seeing the 27 pieces that went in the bin before the final one was created. Remembering that people see things differently they may even have liked one of the 27 you threw away, in fact often it is the pieces that we do not like that others enjoy the most. The audience is not thinking if the hours of planning, practice and research that have gone on to get it to this point and won't notice the little slips and oops marks. In fact it is often these imperfections that make the final piece what it is.

At home my children sometimes put on their jeans and their foot accidently goes through the knee, my 10 year old continues to wear them and calls it a 'style statement'. This is also highly fashionable yet again on the high street. In my twenties I would put a pair of brightly coloured fish net tights underneath my ripped jeans to really draw attention to the holes and the other day I had an amusing moment where I found a pair in a high street store with patches designed to look like pink fishnet tights attached to the inside of the rips. I felt like quite a fashion icon for all of five minutes!

As we become sensible grown-ups we get the urge to fix things in a manner that is invisible or at least less obvious. When we rip our jeans we neatly patch or stitch them back together as invisibly as possible or, for instance, when you accidentally knock Tony's mug out of the cupboard at work and the handle comes off you dash for the superglue, stick it back on and hide it at the back behind someone else's mug before it is missed.

In Japan they take a different approach to accidents and age with a technique called Kintsugi which is used to repair broken pottery and in doing so is felt to make the object even more beautiful than before. This is the epitome of this concept of highlighting an imperfection as the repair is done with gold. The Japanese make a paste with powdered gold and resin and then do one of three things. If it is just cracked the mixture will be used to fill the crack like a thin river of gold running through the side of the pot. If a section is missing it can be rebuilt slowly with the mixture until a whole section of the wall of the pot is then golden. Or finally if a replacement piece can be found to slot into the gap from another broken pot it will be fixed into place with the mixture a bit like a patchwork pot. These are then seen as brand new pots with a whole new lease of life and even more beautiful than they were when they were new.

So just like the pots as you get older you get more beautiful as you gain imperfections. As you have to be repaired you become a new and more beautiful you.

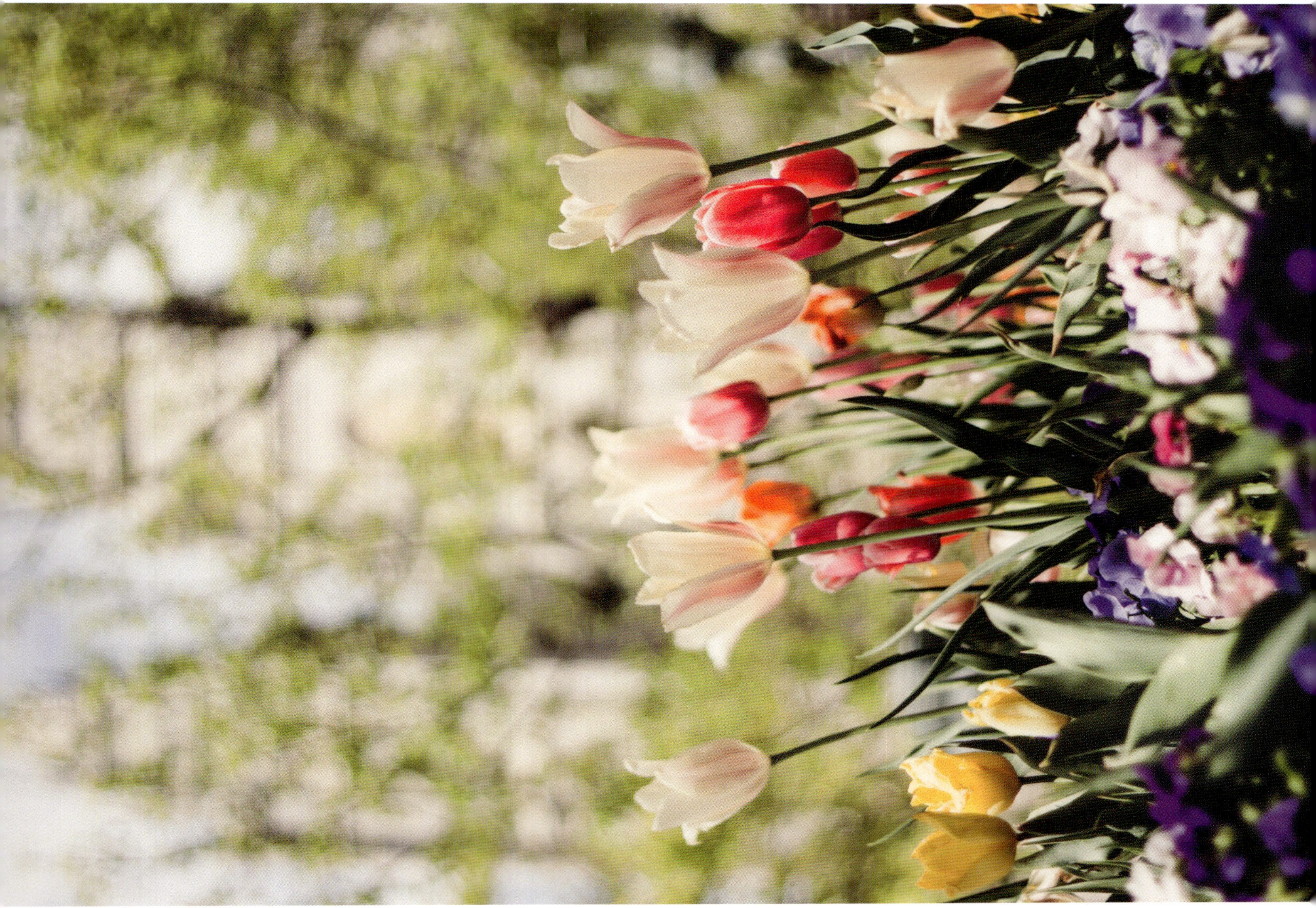

Wabi Sabi style - Let your garden go to seed rather than taming it each year. Nature is designed to look after its own cycle and the flowers will spread naturally through your beds. Go wild with colour too rather than a uniform planting scheme as all the colours of nature are designed to go together.

Celebrating age and wear

Did you embrace the shabby chic movement?

It was a funny moment, in fact some people are still doing it. You take new stuff and some oldish stuff and make it look old/er. It seems ironic really when there is so much old stuff out there to enjoy anyway.

In many cultures age is celebrated in society as there are so many things that come with age that you cannot have with youth. The most important of these is, of course, wisdom. In reverse you cannot have wisdom without age and therefore experience. This comes with its own hazards, one being wear and tear. You live more, you learn more, you wear more. It comes with the deal! You would not be able to accrue this level of knowledge without having lived an interesting life and with this comes the physical reminders of everything you have done. You've all been there for the conversation, this scar is from where I fell off my bike age seven looking for my friends, this is my chicken pox, these stretch marks are baby number three, this is my 'big op' and so it goes on. Then you have general ageing from being outdoors, wearing high heels, walking to work, carrying children/sacks of potatoes and climbing Everest and all the other things you to day to day.

I would argue that it is the fact that we are not perfect that makes us so amazing as the imperfections are the marks of the journey we have taken through life to get us to where we are now, and that journey is not over. You could spend your days sealed up in a box never really ageing, still looking perfect, however you would not get to enjoy your time on this planet. So smile, laugh and keep the lines it makes as a token of the fun you had.

When my eldest was only young he coined the term 'crinkles' for the age lines that started to appear on mummy's face. It says a lot as I was only 24 when I had him. Thankfully the affectionate term for them has stuck as so have the crinkles. Just as we have to embrace the idea that we are not in control of everything in life all the time we have to get comfortable with the idea that we are going to age. Something that makes this easier is that we remind ourselves that everything ages with us.

Are you a bit British? I'm not asking if you have a Bulldog on your arm and drink warm ale! Have you got a collection of family heirlooms that you now keep in a 'bottom drawer', a set of best china for when the Queen comes to tea and clothes kept for 'Sunday best' or, worse still, never worn?

Have you ever considered why you continue to keep these things for special occasions and why you don't use them more often? Does it seem that over the years the special occasions are becoming less frequent and the items are being used less and less. In some families table cloths, china, jewellery and clothing are being passed down to the next generation without ever being used.

My grandmother gave me a lot of very good advice over the years but one of the best was 'there is no point having nice things if you never use them' and I stick to this daily. I use her silver cake slice every time we have cake and her Tiffany salt and pepper set are for everyday use. I get the fancy wine glasses out every time I open a bottle (which is once a month if I'm lucky - four children remember!).

But what if I spill wine on the white table linen or break one of the tea cups I hear you cry.

Let me explain by way of a short story.

Recently I met a lady who had a family table cloth, this table cloth had taken several years and three ladies to hand crochet and had been passed down through three generations yet had never seen the light of day since it was finished as it had spent the whole time in the 'bottom drawer', i.e. that drawer where British families keep the best linen that you only use on special occasions or when the Queen comes to tea. This poor table cloth had never actually been used on a table and was sitting wrapped in tissue paper not even being looked at after all that time had been spent making it. The lady had just listen to me giving a talk about Wabi Sabi and had realised that the cloth was still ageing even hidden away not being used. She had come to the realisation that, yes, there was the risk that wine might get spilt on the cloth, it might need a clean, but at least it would finally be fulfilling the purpose that the ladies had spent all those years making it for. She was going to go home and put it on the table and enjoy it.

Fabrics age. Yes even in the bottom drawer, in the wardrobe or in the cupboard. If you do not get them out and use them they will eventually just become tatters on their own and they will never have been enjoyed.

The problem is often that we endow the objects in our possession with so much value that we become too scared to use them. We actually put more value into them than the original owner as they start to feel irreplaceable once that person is no longer with us. Sometimes we may not even be keeping them because we like them but purely because they used to belong to someone who we no longer have in our lives. When they were made it was to be a functional object. Just because the process involved was longer and the materials seemingly more valuable to us in our modern society of plastics and throwaway, cheap products, we avoid using it. Our ancestors were able to remove a stain and they did not have access to the detergents we have now so I'm sure if Aunt Lily spills red wine on it you can get it right back out again. And if you cannot and it leaves a slight mark it is not the end of the world.

Take a look in your wardrobe, this can be one of the worst places for this. How many of the things in there are you not wearing because 'it's not quite the right occasion'. Make an occasion, or more to the point you don't need an occasion. Why can't you go to the supermarket in your ballgown (if you don't own one then you need one on your life - substitute for tuxedo if more suitable) It's only you that is saying that it is not appropriate not to. So next time you're off to your choice of local food store put your glad rags on and enjoy your shop, you can even dance down the aisles while you do it. The other shoppers will only look at you oddly because they will wish they had done the same. I do recommend sensible footwear though as cornering in high heels with a full trolley is

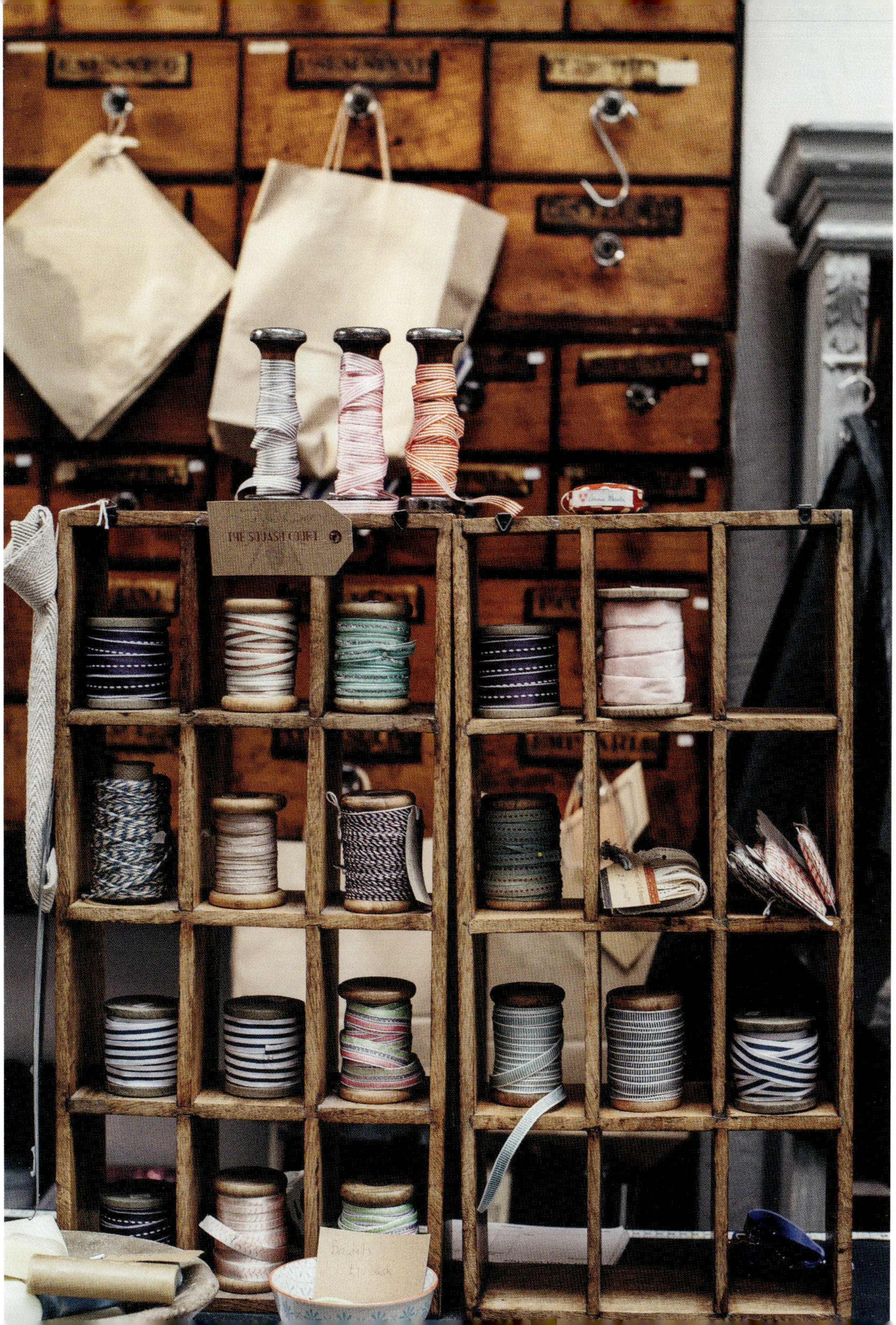

Wabi Sabi style - They may be beautiful, but do not just collect them, use them. If you do not they will just decay anyway until the fibres are no longer strong enough and then it is too late.

really difficult. Maybe everyday does not need to be a jeans and t.shirt day. Have you just got into the habit of wearing them because it is easy and they are comfortable? Why not wear something nice for a change. If you are not about to go wading through a swamp then put on your best frock, get some nice jewellery out, dig out the flamingo patterned shirt, don the top hat, what have you got to lose? If you do not wear it today when will you?

While we are on the topic of things ageing even though you are not using them - Do you have a stash? Collection of things to make stuff with, finishing making, do...?

When you look at this collection I'm sure you have things you are happy to just hack into and use, tools that get used the most, items that get happily used up and reused again and again. Then there are the special bits. The paints, fabrics, papers, kits, tools, whatevers that you have that you cannot quite bring yourself to use just yet. This project is not quite good enough for them, I'll just wait until next time, I'll just do this one first. All these thoughts go through your mind each time you look at them and they never quite make it to the doing pile. You think you love them just that little bit too much to use them.

We moved house a couple of years ago and the stash moved with us. Because I make for a living it is not small either. In my stash I found fabric I had bought in college which was a couple of years ago (ok, about 20) and I started to wonder why I had not used it. First I used the age old excuse of 'I've not found the right project yet'. In all that time I'm sure the right project has come and gone more than once so that is not it. So I tried the next, it's not quite good enough... and then I realised that actually what we are all saying to ourselves when we look at these things that we cannot bring ourselves to use is that we think *we* are not good enough to use *them*. Now this is a whole new ball game.

I have a friend who has a button, It's her favourite button. She has had this button for twenty years. She gets it out every now and then and looks at it and says. 'ah, what a nice button'. Then she puts it away again. If she had put that button on a bag or a coat or a hat she could have enjoyed that button every day for years until, yes, it would have eventually worn out and then she would have been able to get a new favourite button out and replace it and enjoy that one too. Instead she has had a few minutes in all these years.

It is only a thing. It can be replaced. Get it out and use it. Yes even the shibori fabric you bought in Japan, the bag handle from your tour of India, the paper you made on your course last year and the hand made Chinese brushes you got for Christmas. Just like the ballgown, the tuxedo and the tea set, it needs to be used. Yes, once you use it will start to wear but then you will actually get to enjoy it more. So, if you wear your ballgown and it gets a slight mark or hole and needs a repair you can patch it with one of your favourite fabrics from your stash and then it will be even more beautiful. If you do not use it you run the risk of your stash turning into another British heirloom and dooming it to someone else's bottom drawer. Remember, ***You* are good enough *everyday*.**

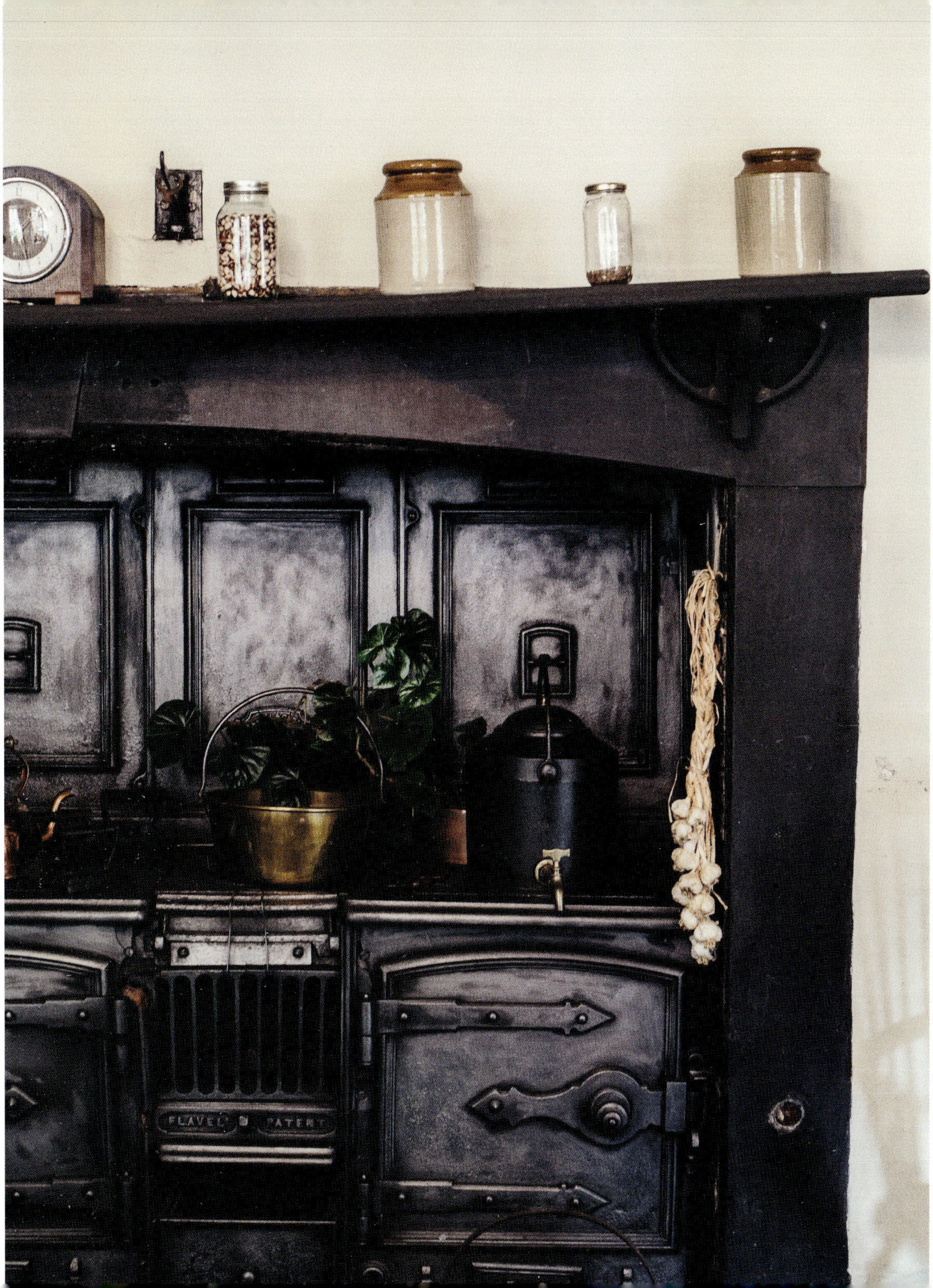

Wabi Sabi style - Wonky and old is beautiful. Let the age of the object shine through and do not whitewash it or cover it over with modern fittings, enjoy the rich history it brings.

Project - The Art of Mending

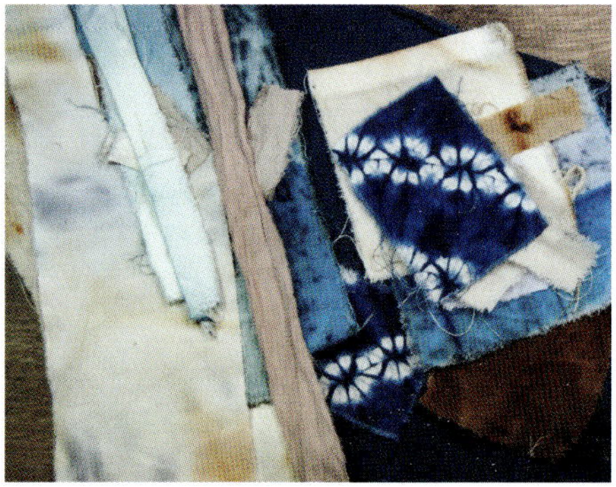

Making does not have to be a process of always working with something new. Wabi Sabi is about loving what we already have and learning to work with it, you can enjoy the artful results that come from mending and fixing techniques. Inspired by the beautiful Boro quilts of Japan you can mend and darn your way to something new and beautiful from something old or scraps.

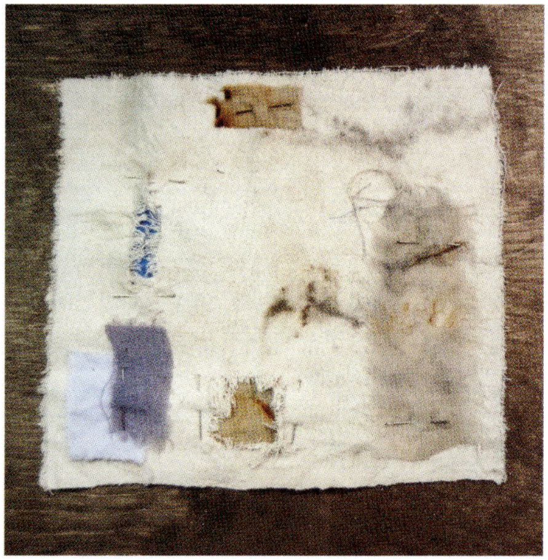

Start by collecting together a selection of pieces of fabric. Offcuts, preloved and worn sections, hand dyed, stained, torn, household linen, old clothing, it will all be perfect for this project. It will finally be stitched together into a book so decide on a page size. I have chosen c. 20x20cm square. You may prefer to cut out all your book pages in one go or work one at a time - it's up to you. Once you have your backing fabric you can then start to lay top patches on and pin in place once you are happy with the arrangement. The idea is to rebuild the backing page so pay attention to worn areas or create your own if there are none by cutting holes and fraying the edges.

The background can also be created from more than one piece of fabric, especially if you do not have enough of your chosen piece to make all your pages. Consider if you want all the pages to be the same colour, if you want a colour theme or if you like randomness.

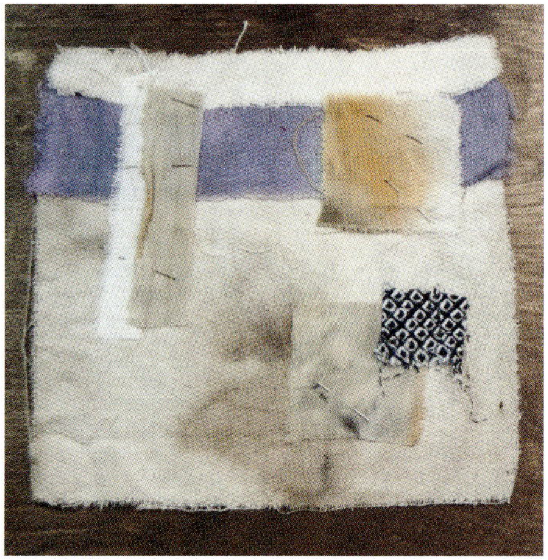

When you are choosing your thread, vary it so that sometimes it blends with the fabrics and sometimes it contrasts. You don't have to use embroidery thread, crochet cotton is great as it unravels less as you sew, fine yarn works too. You can even pull strands of the weave from the edges of your fabric and sew with these for a really authentic feel. This mixture of threads will give a more relaxed feel to the piece. Do not always stitch in the same direction when attaching the patches, go with what feels most comfortable for each one.

To give the impression that the fabric has been fixed and mended over time you need to stitch on the bottom patch first, yes the one that is under the others just to be awkward, completely covering it in stitches or just stitching the edges down. Just remember to do the whole patch even where you won't see the stitching when the next patch is sewn on. The layers of stitch will build as you put the next fabric on top and it adds depth and texture. Slightly sheer fabrics allow the lower layers of stitch and fabric to show through too and would show if you had not completed the stitching.

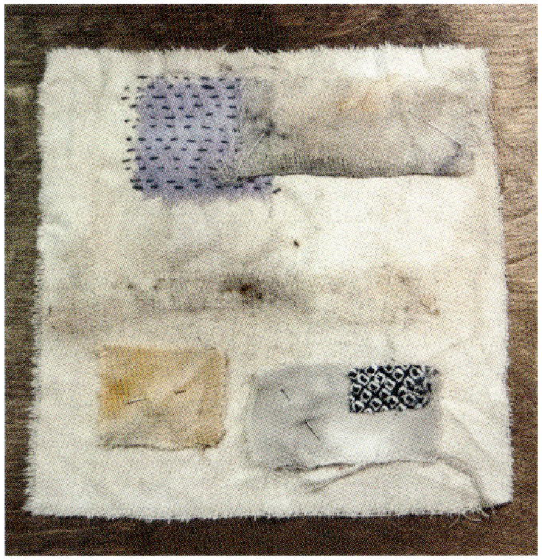

Consider whip stitch edges, lines of running stitch, cross shaped stitches. Try traveling in one or two directions on a patch. When patching holes make sure the edges are well secured.

Once you have finished your single pages you can then attach them together in pairs. Pin them back to back and pick a thread that matches the background colour on your page. My pages are alternate blue and 'white' so as I stitch in the background thread on one page it is a great contrast on the reverse. I have followed around the edges of my patches on the side that matches the thread making a seemingly random line on the other page which adds character whilst holding the two pages together.

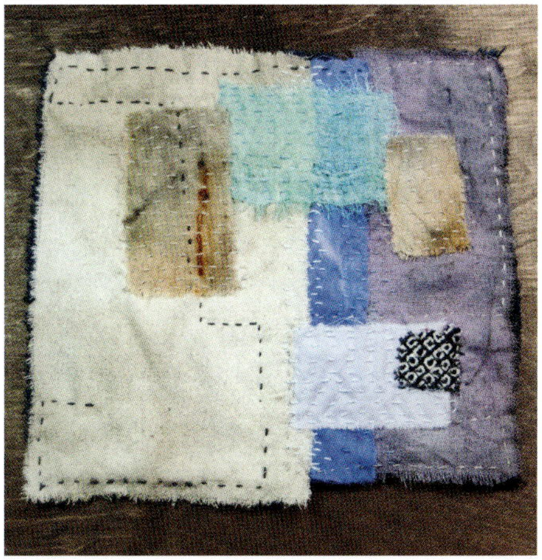

This stitching is a holding stitch and needs to travel around the edges of the pages and across the middle so the pages do not sag apart. You can also use a whip or blanket stitch to hold any loose edges together if you like.

Once your pairs are complete place together in a pile and pin/clamp along the 'spine'. Now choose a good strong thread and whip stitch or blanket stitch along the length of the spine making sure you have caught all the pages in each stitch.

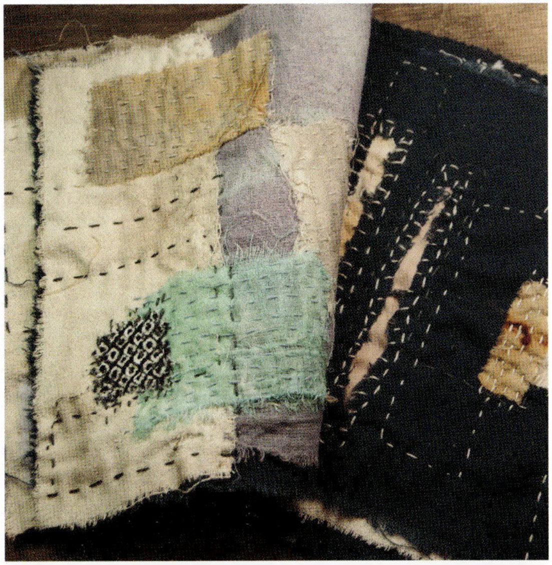

The best thing about a textile book is you can add extra pages whenever you like, so keep making. You can also continue to stitch into the pages once they are in the book.

You could also get creative and join them in a line, page by page, and make a concertina book instead.

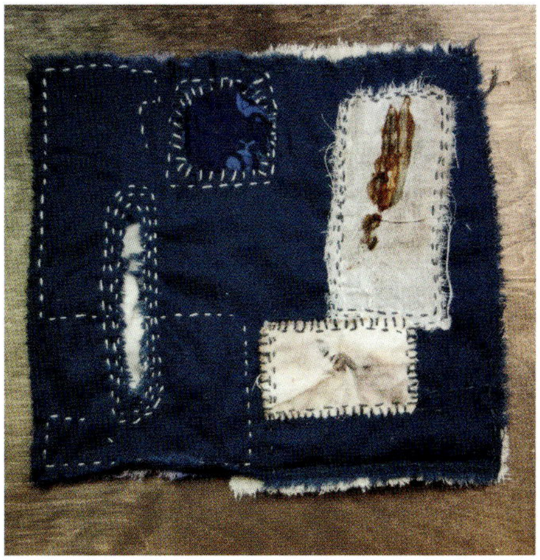

Simplicity and economy

Not everything needs to be a Louis the XIV four poster bed (It would be wonderful sometimes, but hard work everyday). A simple linen apron dress, a nice pair of woolly socks, a good pair of garden shears. Appreciating simple quality and the ability to mend not throw away and buy new. The clothing industry is one of the most polluting in the world. We have become a culture where clothing is also seen as throw away for women, men and children. Homewares too, from decorations and art to garden furniture and appliances are not designed to last and instead of fixing we are programmed to dispose of them and get more. Fashion in all areas of our lives drives changes throughout our houses, gardens and workplaces and we need to stop and take check of what we are doing.

The idea of repairing instead of replacing is not a new one. In Britain through necessity we had the government issue Make Do and Mend movement during the war when new items and materials were at an all-time low so as a nation we were urged to fix everything, so we could continue to support the war effort with every possible resource. This also drove new avenues in design. Manufacture without waste. Function was at the forefront in all object design while retaining style. These objects are now coveted as retro and minimalist, harking back to an era where life seemed less complicated. Once the furniture rationing ended in 1952, people relaxed, design flourished and life became more plastic and disposable driving forwards to the society we know today.

An excellent example of mending through necessity is Japanese Boro quilts. These quilts were passed through many generations of a family and were patched together to keep them alive. In Japan this stitching is called Sashiko and at the time it was for purely functional purposes, lines of running stitch often overlapping and whip stitched edges designed to hold the new patches of fabric in place and keep the fibres of the old fabrics together. The quilts are predominantly tones of natural linen and shades of blue as the main dye available at the time was indigo, however other tones appear where whatever fabrics were available have been used to keep the quilt alive. This same technique was also used on clothing like jackets. Over the years Sashiko stitching has evolved to be less functional and it has developed into a more decorative form. Ironically these quilts are now worth hundreds of pounds and are highly sought after, as are the types of fabrics that from which they are made.

In India a similar style of functional stitch is called Kantha and is a simple running stitch used to join layers of fabric together. This is used to repurpose sari silk into other items when they become too worn. In the UK our word for this style of stitching is decidedly less sexy.... Darning.

The key to Wabi Sabi is to be happy with what you have rather than constantly yearning for more. The ability to think of creative ways to use items already in your home goes hand in hand with this. If you need a plant pot and you cannot find one what do you have that will serve the same purpose? Just because something was not designed and labelled as 'plant pot' does not mean it cannot function as one. The same is true of your supplies for making. Just because a piece of fabric

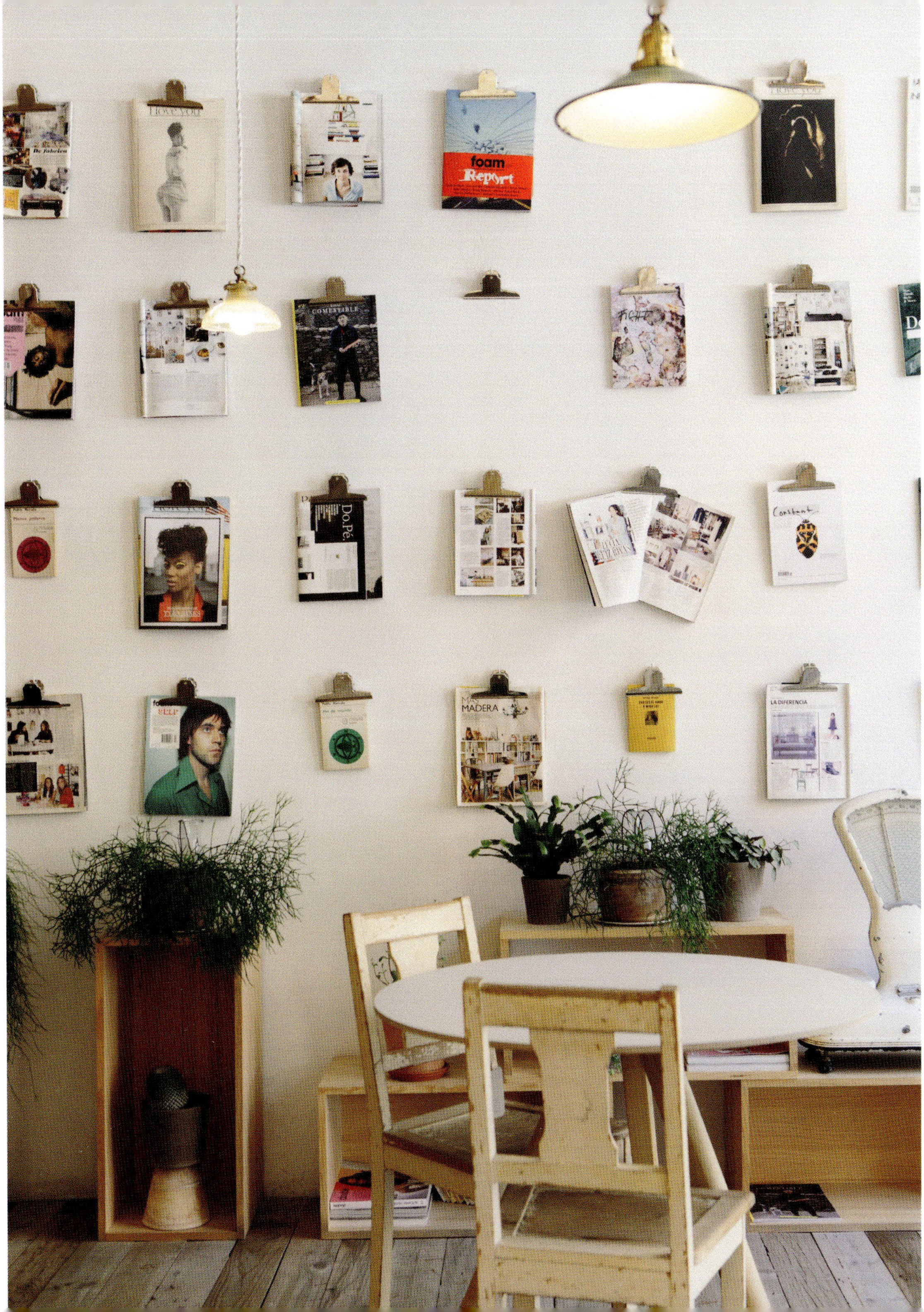

Wabi Sabi style - hang your favourite magazines, prints, pictures, drawings or whatever you like on bulldog clips to make your wall into a gallery or library and change them as often as you like.

says dress fabric on it does not mean you cannot make a bag from it and similarly you can make a dress from a pair of curtains. All it takes is some Wabi Sabi spirit and a little imagination.

The art of letting go

Why is it harder to let go of things than we have put time into than things we have just bought? For instance, why can we throw away that mug that we picked up at the supermarket with a catchy slogan that we no longer find relevant, but we cannot get rid of the painting we did 10 years ago that hangs on the living room wall that we hated even when we did it!

Marie Kondo taught us that we could finally let go of the dress we had never worn as it had taught us that actually we were never meant to wear dresses like that in the first place and for me keeping it was a daily reminder of the fact that I wouldn't wear it. She did it purely by getting us to look at what we have and getting us to ask do we really like it? Ok so this does not mean we get to throw out our accounts and the vacuum cleaner too, but it does mean we have to use a different set of eyes on our life. This was part of the moment where I realised that I needed to start wearing my ballgown as I loved it so much but had not worn it. However, it is hard to apply this theory when you have personally invested so much in something but still cannot find a love or a use for it.

We have spent years of our life working to get to where we are now, and we feel we have put in too much effort doing what we do to give up on it. It feels like we are admitting defeat to stop and therefore we keep on going rather than having the strength to say that actually we would be better off stopping and starting something new. This starts with simple things like paintings, cooking even watching films. Wabi Sabi teaches us that life is about an ongoing cycle that never ends so sometimes it is ok to stop doing something and move on to new pastures in order to continue that cycle.

Lets look at our creative side first. When we are making we often feel we have to complete everything we started. This is habitually installed from our school days where we are taught that we have to finish all our artworks. We are made to feel bad about having a pile of WIP's/UFO's or whatever you call them. Do you feel like you never really get time to finish anything? Look back over the last twelve months and I am sure you have finished things, the important things, the things you enjoyed the most. The other things did not need to be done yet. What we need to understand is that everything in life is a learning process - there should be no such thing as a regret for we are the person we are today by everything we have done up to this moment. The same is true of our creative processes. There is no need to finish everything you start, it is ok to admit something is not working and stop making it! You have learnt from the process and can now start again having made progress and can do better with the next one. Some things are never meant to be finished.... Ever.

My WIP pile often becomes my 'ooh, I can turn that into something else pile.' If I have not returned

Wabi Sabi style - go through your wardrobe and decide what you love and wear it. If it gets a hole, fix it and wear it again. If you do not love it, use it for something else or give it to someone.

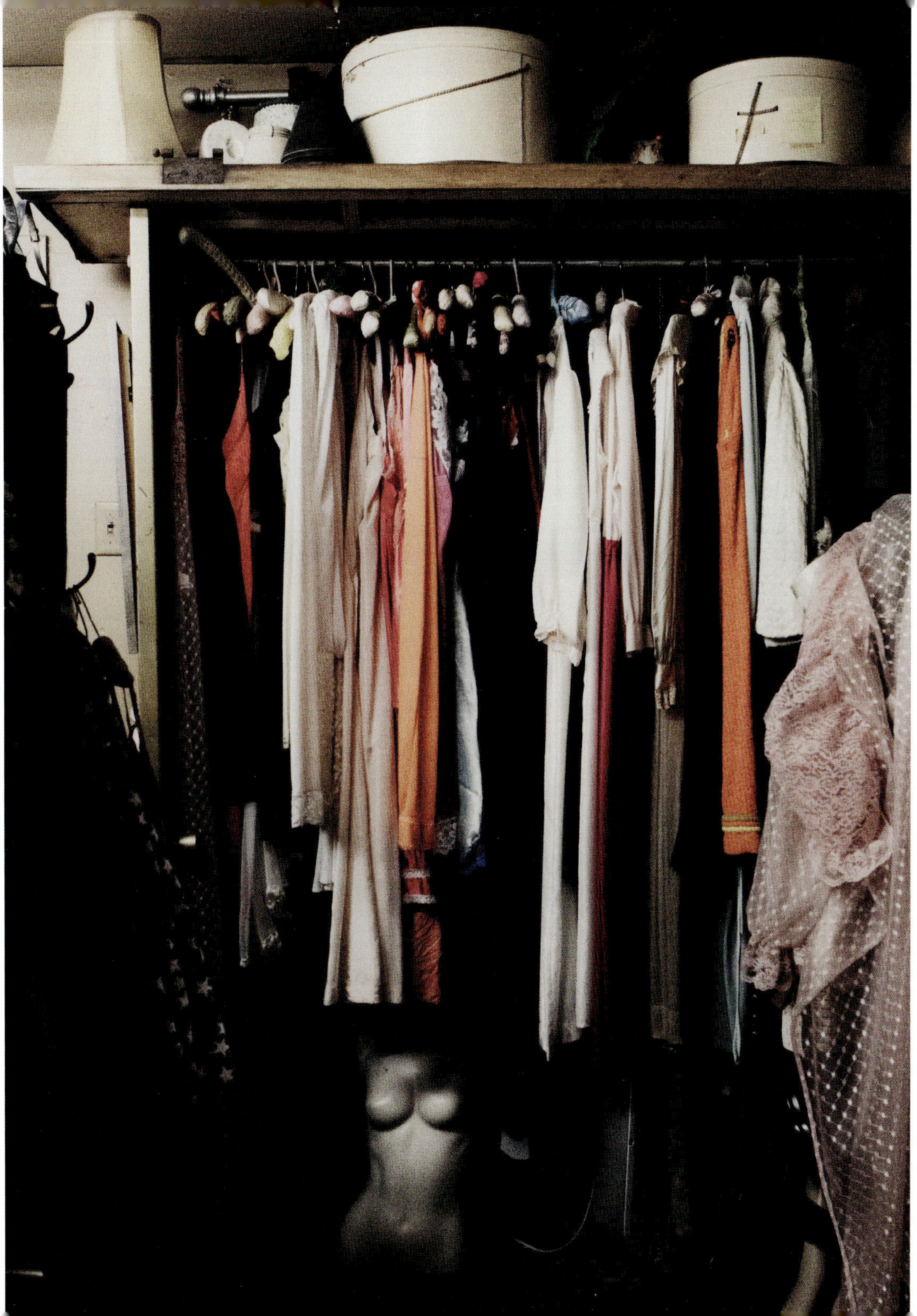

Project - Your workspace

Does your workspace currently look a little like this?

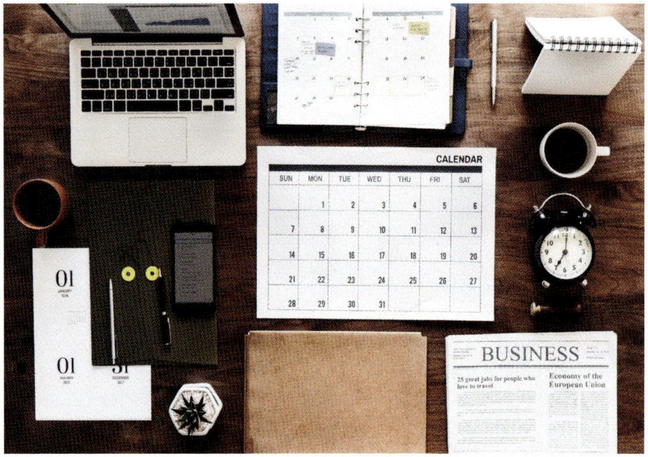

Then lets see what we can do...

It is nice and orderly but not at all Wabi Sabi! You can still be organised but let the calming influence in. Lets start with the fact that you are doing too much at once, the calendar, the diary, the phone, the computer, it's all on the go at the same time. Focus on one thing at a time and set yourself a limit. Most creative people work from home or balance a life of day job and creative job so try to do more hours than actually exist - manage them carefully and you can do it.

Remove some of the items from the desk. Some of these are duplicates, do you really need a diary and a calendar? If so, synchronise once a week. Put the phone away, if it rings and you are busy decided if you really need to answer it right now or if you can call them back. If the computer does not need to be on turn it off, not sleep mode, OFF. It saves the environment and money.

Avoid social media except when on designated breaks and if you use it for work set a time limit. No more then 30 minutes across an entire day is plenty to get your message out there. Remember to STOP. Working from home, or more than one role, promotes the inability to set a sensible work life balance. You need to have down time too, so make sure you still have evenings and days off.

Bring in a few Wabi Sabi touches, they were always there traditionally, nature in the form of a pot plant, a photo of your loved ones, some inspiring objects. Make your desk feel friendly and, most importantly, make room for you. If you need more space use a bookshelf or pinboard. You need to feel happy while you are in your space so when you are having a blank, uninspired moment you can look around and feel calmed and motivated.

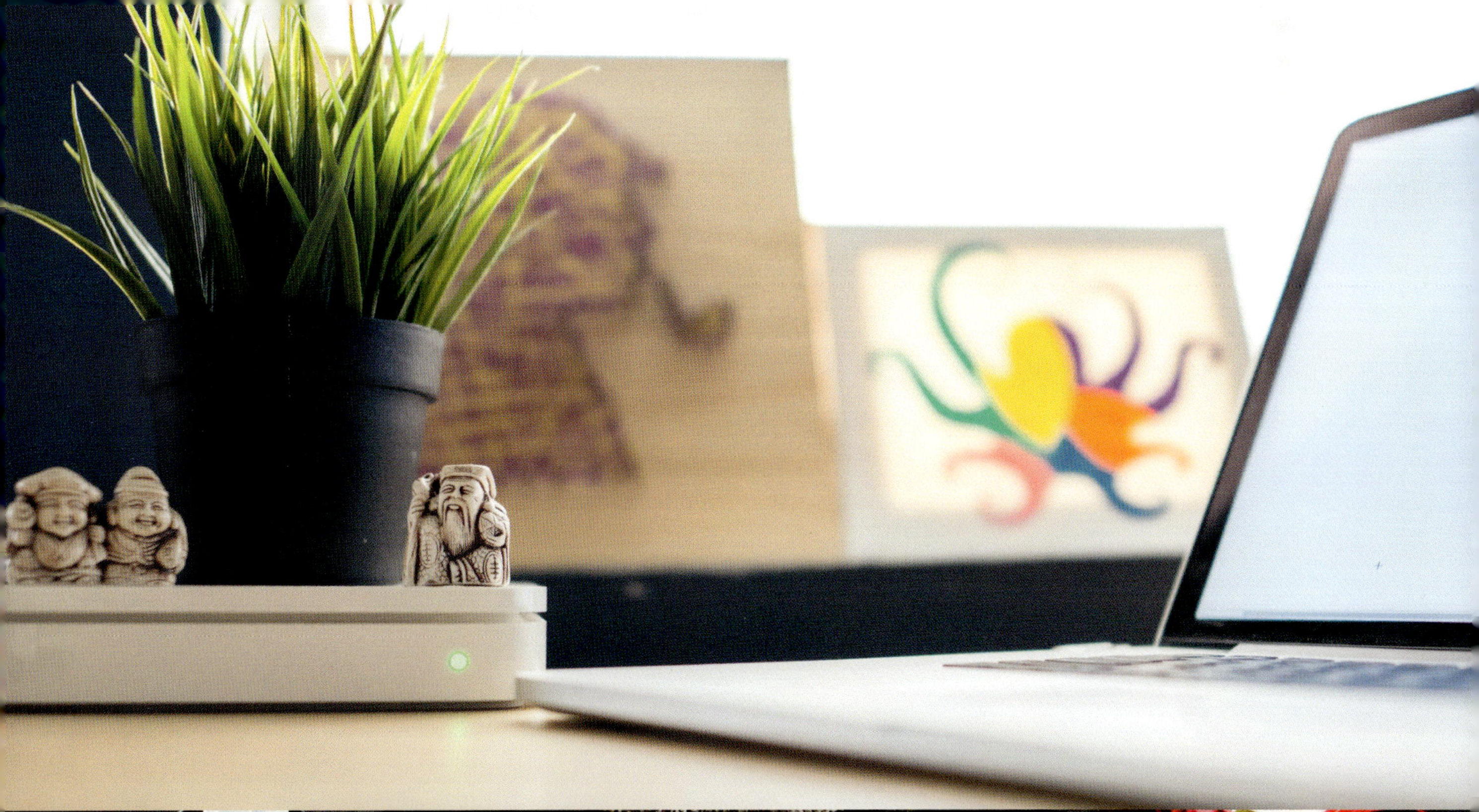

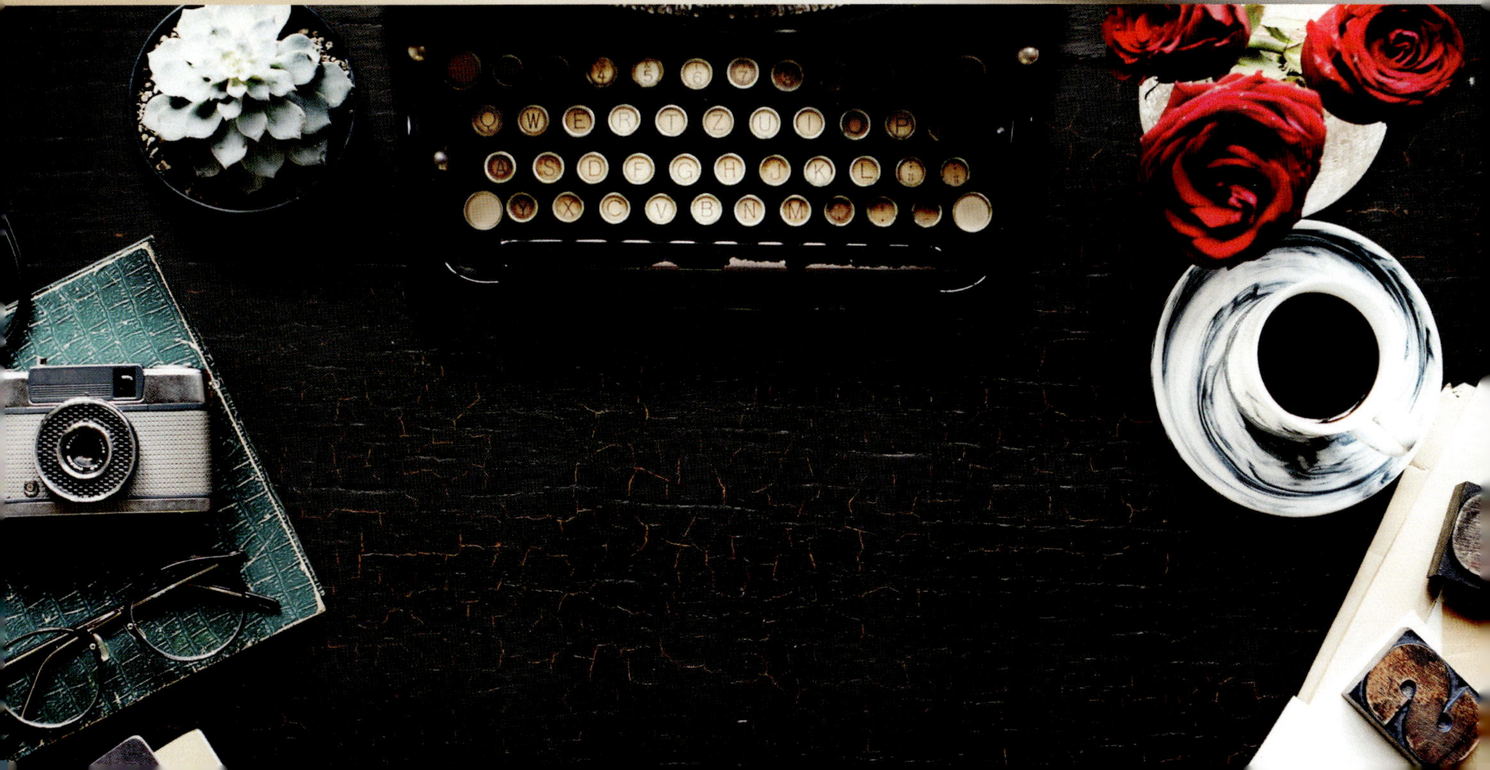

to a piece after a long time then I am happy to say I am not going to. And if a piece makes me annoyed when I am working on it, I stop working on it.

This can also be applied to the wider aspects of our life. Sometimes we soldier on with jobs we hate or roles we feel an obligation to because we have been doing them for so long we feel we have invested too much of ourselves in them to give up on them. Rethink that idea, you are not giving up on them; you are realising that they have served their purpose in your life and now you need to move on to something new.

Sketchbooks, a quick thought...

These are the worst place for feeling to need to finish when all you need to do is use them. They are for storing ideas, having inspirational moments, collecting images and words, doodles, thoughts, postcards, stamps, leaflets, notes, printing off your photographs and, dare I say it, sketches! Paint, draw, print, stitch. Use paper, fabric, metal, wood. Have a book, a concertina fold or just loose leaves. They are not for masterpieces, nor are they an artwork in their own right. Be free to use them (or not) however you want and never, ever compare yours to anyone else's.

Seeing mistakes as new directions

How many times do you start something and when you get to the end it's not what you aimed for?

To most people this concludes with 'oh my word, what a waste of time'. (or something less polite) In all we are not very good at being nice to ourselves when faced with what we see as failure.

> 'I've not failed. I've just found 10,000 ways that won't work'

Edison was talking about his research when trying to make the lightbulb. He didn't see it as failure, it was a path he had to take on the way to making the discovery. He realised we cannot expect to get everything right on our first try and that it often takes time; trial and effort.

The other thing that comes from mistakes is new directions. Happy accidents they sometimes get called. They may not be what you had been aiming for on the day in question, but they are a valid direction. You may never follow the direction and you may not even keep the result, but what you are doing is coming up with a positive outcome rather than a negative one. So back to where we were listening to our music in the M6 carpark and loving the extra time to do so because we have reframed the situation. The mistake is not a mistake it is a new idea, an alternative route, a possible different direction, but not a fail.

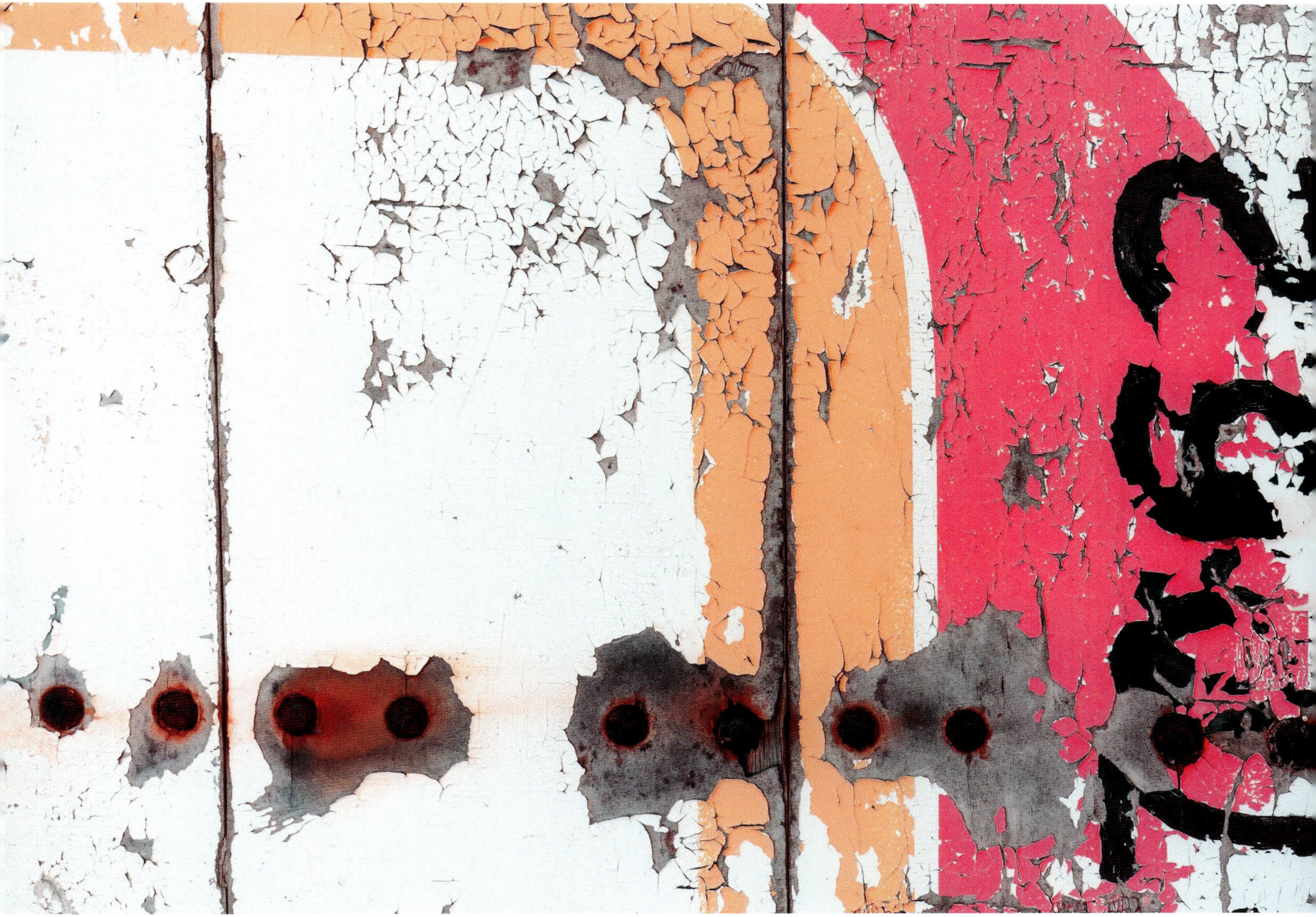

Wabi Sabi style - Let the years of age and weathering show through. The texture created by the paint peeling back from the surface of the metal adds depth and character to this surface that would not have existed when it was new. The rust also adds a new depth of colour and softens the edges.

Project - Rewriting mistakes

Here is your chance to realise some mistakes and work out how they were not really mistakes at all.... (these can be in your work or life)

List the mistake on this page and how they could be a new direction on the opposite page

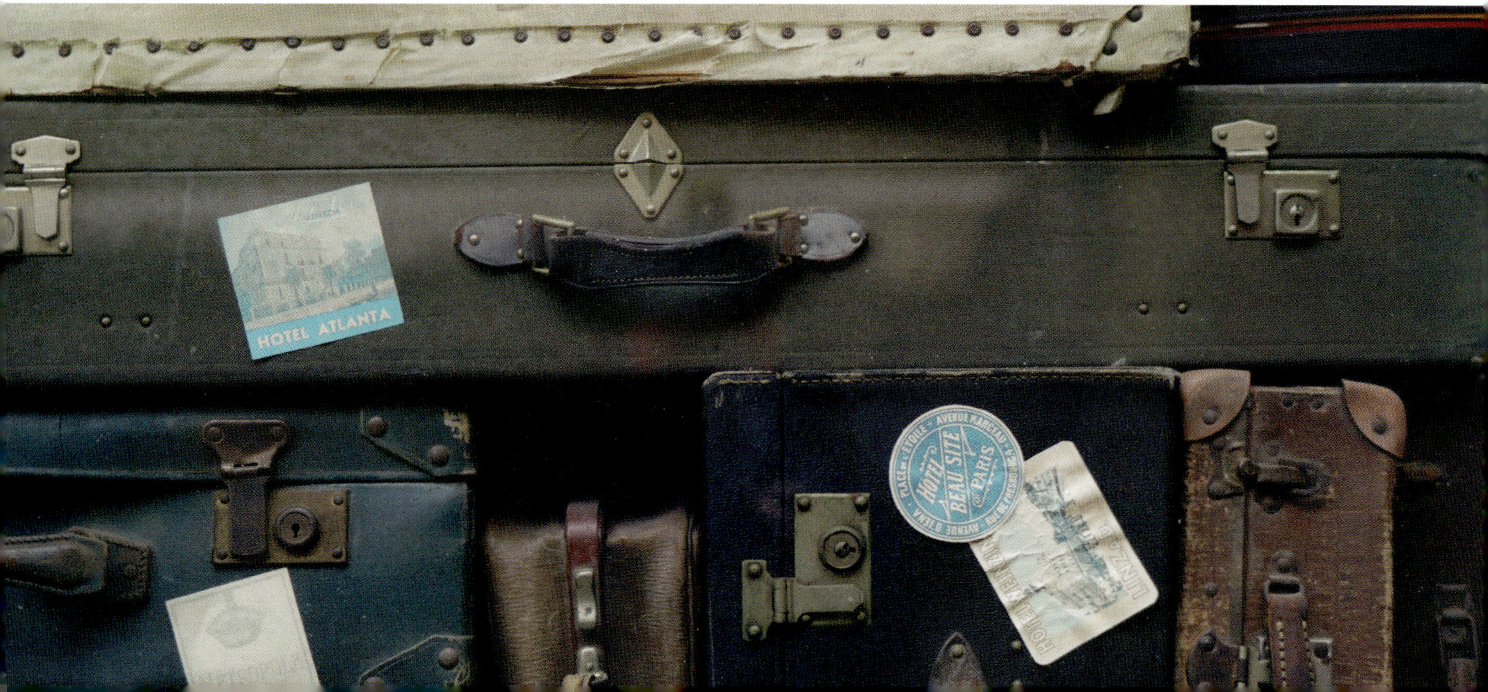

Once you start to reframe mistakes as positive moments they become more manageable. It opens up new avenues in your work/life and enables you to experiment more.

This will, in turn, create more learning opportunities and your work/life will progress, diversify and be more enjoyable.

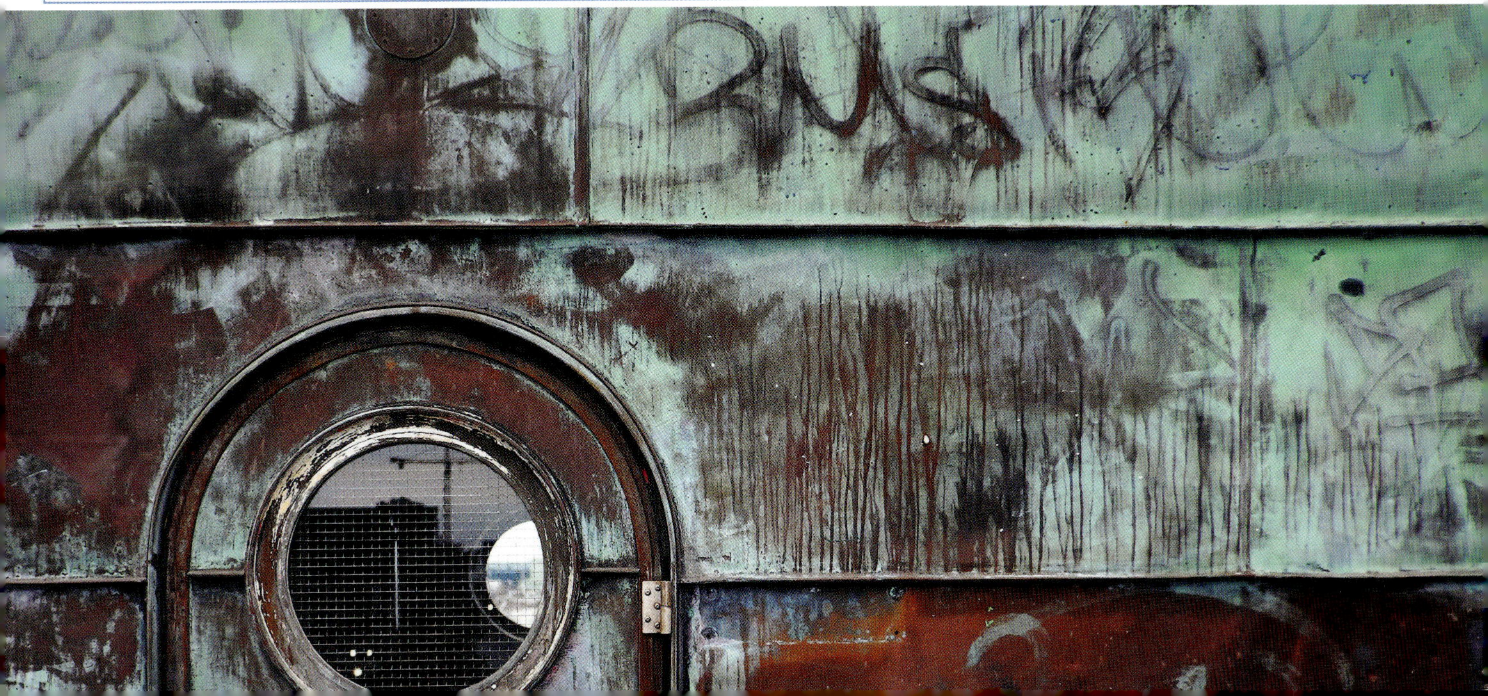

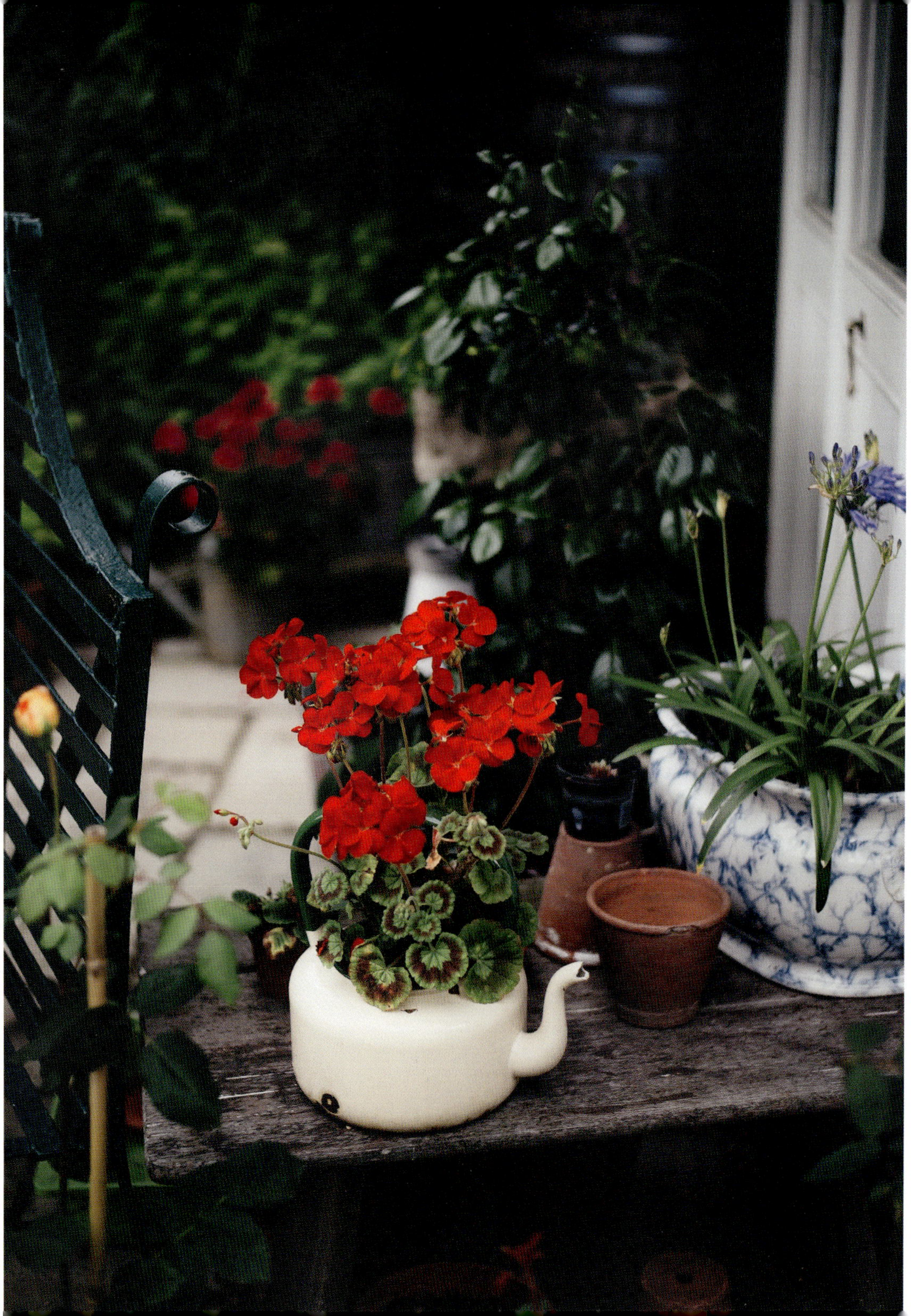

Wabi Sabi style - Why use a traditional planter when a tea pot or something more interesting will do. Get creative with your gardening and use anything you like, just remember to make drainage holes in the bottom if it will live outdoors otherwise it could become waterlogged.

Having mentored professional Artists for years one thing I always have to remind them is that not every piece you start will be a masterpiece that you can sell for millions and that you should not push yourself to think that it should be or you will only let yourself down on a regular basis. This will make you feel worse about your achievements and lower your self-esteem. Those 27 tries that you threw in the bin were a learning experience. Do not throwing them away, stop look at them. Is there anything in them that you could work with. Just because today you aimed to create a seascape and it came out looking like the Sahara Desert, does not mean you despair, put it to one side as next week you might want to do an arid scene. So your dye went pink when you rinsed it not the lovely ruby red it looked like in the bath, overdye it, it's all the rage at the moment. The model's legs came out too long at life drawing, go home and study Giacommetti it might start a whole new series.

The same goes for anything in life. If you are trying to start something new you cannot expect to be good at it from day one. It takes time and practice to improve and we all have off days too. If it's not working stop for the day and try something else. Yes, even at your day job it is ok to say I need to take five minutes and have a breather as this is not working at the moment. It's like spending hours trying to figure out the last pieces of a puzzle and your brain eventually cannot see the wood for the trees, take a break come back in a bit and often it all clicks into place.

About relaxing and enjoying what you do

You only live once so you need to enjoy it.

Life is getting ever faster. We all need to slow down.

Did you know that one of the biggest causes of stress in the workplace is emails? This is because people feel that because they come in instantly they need to be replied to instantly. This is not the case. When communication only came by post we did not have to reply to a letter instantly. We had in trays and out trays and lost somewhere in between space! We filed things and did them in the correct order of importance, not just because some irate lady kept hitting the send button. Who cares if you respond within 15 minutes to messages on Facebook, so you can get the fast badge? Does this mean you will live longer?

Britain and Japan now have two of the most stressed and overworked populations in the world. We work some of the longest hours, push our minds and bodies to the limit and for what?

We need to stop and create 'me time'. Becoming engrossed in a creative activity activates our parasympathetic nervous system which means that our sympathetic nervous system (our anxiousness) is deactivated. Or to put it more simply, if you activate the creative doing side of your brain to the point where you are truly engaged with the creative activity, you know that moment when you look at your watch and think 'ooh heck, where did the last hour go?', the stress side is overridden; incapable of being active at the same time.

Project - Mindful Stitching

Being mindful is about being in the moment and allowing nothing else to matter. Do whatever helps you with this - put on some music, have a cup of tea, curl up on the sofa, as long as you have everything to hand and you are comfortable before you start.

The idea is to concentrate on the stitching and the fabric and let the worries of life fade away. You know you have cracked it when you look at the time and think 'ooh, where did the last hour go?'.

Follow these simple guidelines for selecting the right types of fabric:

Base fabric needs to be felt or batting (firm but soft!) this gives a good stability to the piece and is kind to your hands. You can always use another piece of thinner fabric like cotton as a backing too if you prefer a lighter weight finish to your work.

Top fabrics should be soft enough to stitch through by hand, think light weight cotton and synthetics, silks and linen. Old clothes and off cuts are a great source of pieces for this as you only need small bits plus this adds a personal touch to your individual pieces.

Finishing touches can be vintage and specialist fabrics as you only need small pieces. I love to use Japanese fabrics as this technique pays homage to the Japanese technique of Boro quilting, however other cultures also use similar techniques and Indian sari silk or Indonesian wood block prints would look equally striking.

> Do not overthink your fabric layout as it is a background for the stitching. It can feel quite plain and disjointed until the stitches bring it all together.

Place down your backing then lay out your plainer fabrics. You can keep them as large pieces or cut them smaller if you like. Try not to end up with too many layers to stitch through at once as this will make the process more difficult.

Next use your patterned and textured pieces of fabric to finish covering the background. Overlap the pieces and don't worry too much about the layout

Finally take your detail fabric pieces, cut small and place these on top to finish your composition. This is a great way to use your favourite treasured pieces that you could never part with.

You can hold you pieces in place with pins, tacking stitches or my favourite is iron on fusing web as this allows you to stitch away without worry of stabbing yourself and with all your fabrics secured in place from the beginning.

Keep the stitches simple - My work (shown opposite) only uses running stitch (up and down in straight lines). You can run the stitches as close together or far apart as you like and they do not have to be regular. The lines do not even have to be that straight. You can work the whole piece at once or just focus on small sections at a time if you like.

You can use all sorts of thread and the biggest needle you have. Embroidery strands, silks, wool, crochet cotton, linen or whatever you enjoy stitching with. Consider your choice of colour. A neutral colour will flatten out the piece if used all the way across but leave the fabric as the focus. A bold colour will draw attention to the thread. You can vary your thread colour changing to suit each section of fabric or simply switch each time your strand runs out.

Use your thread either as it is or, if it is stranded, split it into three strand pieces for a finer look. I prefer to work with a thinner thread so that the fabrics are the dominant factor in the piece, but the choice is yours. Keep your thread short. Do not cut pieces that are longer than the distance from your hand to your elbow or it will become distressed and then so will you! When your thread runs out just knot it off at the back by passing the needle back through your loop and pulling tight then start again from where you finished. No-one will see the back so it does not matter what it looks like.

Imperfections are the key to this technique. Allow your stitches to be wonky and your lines to wobble. It adds character and charm, but most importantly, you can relax and just enjoy doing it.

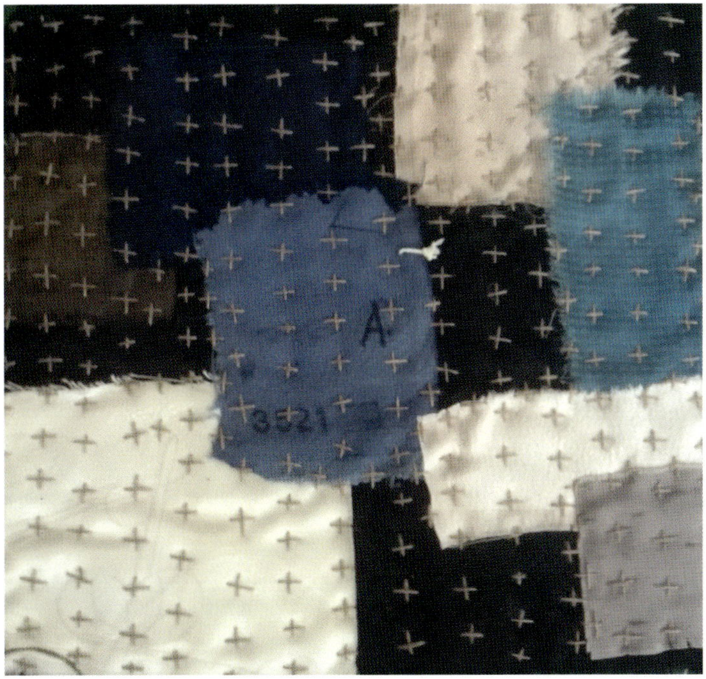

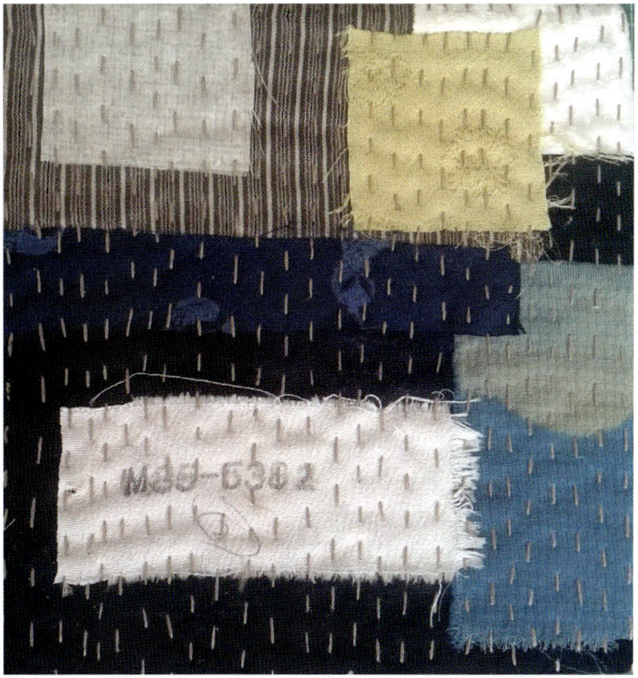

Make more, stress less and live longer. Whatever it is you like doing you should do it. It has to be an activity that does not induce stress in the doing though. I have a friend who gets more stressed by trying to knit than not so this won't work for her but might for you. Complicated, counted cross stitch is generally out, as is anything involving numerous rows, fine tweezers or magnifying glasses. Something simple and repetitive works best.

The Wabi Sabi effect

Once you start to truly embrace your Wabi Sabi you begin to look at the world differently. Things you used to walk past everyday that would blend into the background will catch your eye. You will find beauty in the simple things in life. I am often found taking photographs of crumbling walls and textured floors. My Macro lens is my favourite as it brings to life even the simplest object.

You stop making excuses for not using things and start to enjoy them everyday as *you* are worth it, not just the Queen and as this feeling becomes more normal you lose the urge to rush out and buy new things as you already have everything you need. So when you do buy anything you appreciate it more.

Junk shops and car boot sales will become your favourite shopping places. You will never be able to say no when someone has something that needs a new home if you can find a reason to use it (as if you can say no already as a crafter anyway!)

Your outlook on life is more positive, calmer and in line with nature. Your home and your garden will slowly become one and the same, interchanging objects between the two will be more normal. Making time in your life to do what *you* want and a space in which to do it will become important not an aside and you will not feel guilty for doing so.

You also begin to have exciting ideas. I am sure as you flick through your social media stream you have come across ideas like those you have seen through out the book and you hit the like button. Someone out there had to have those ideas, photograph them and post them online. Now you are embracing your inner Wabi Sabi why should it not be you.

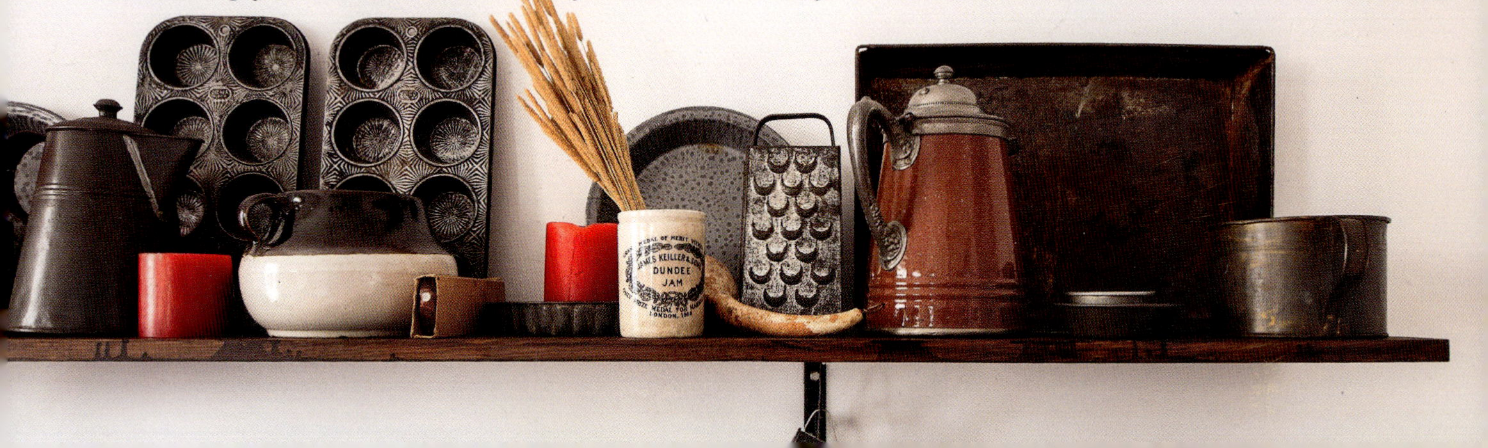

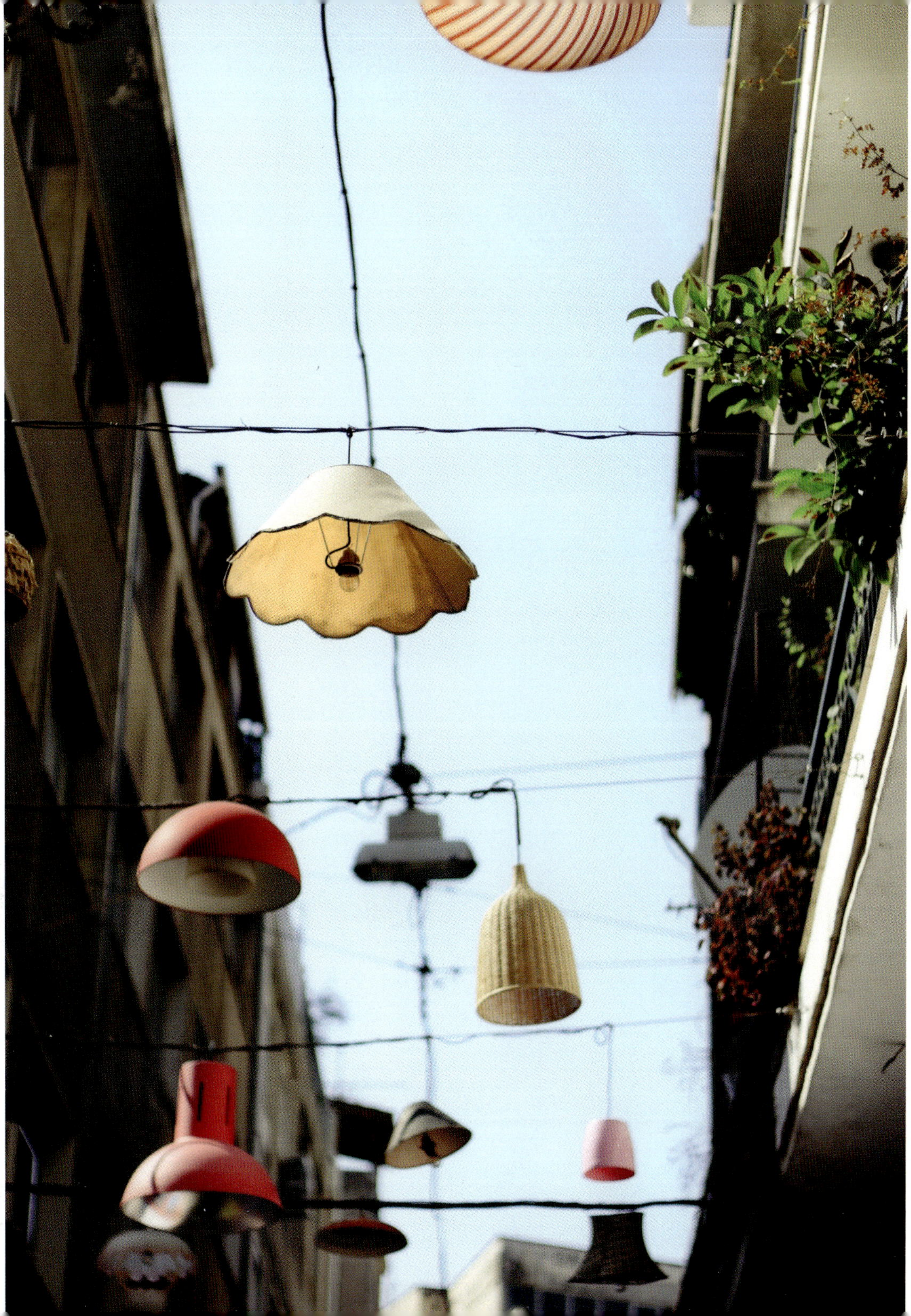

Wabi Sabi style - Objects where you do not expect to see them. Indoor lighting outdoors - we worry about things getting damaged because they were not designed to be used outdoors, yet they look so beautiful you will have as much enjoyment from them outside as inside, so just go for it.

Project - Wabi Sabi mood board

Start your own Wabi Sabi inspiration board. Find something to stick your ideas to and start.

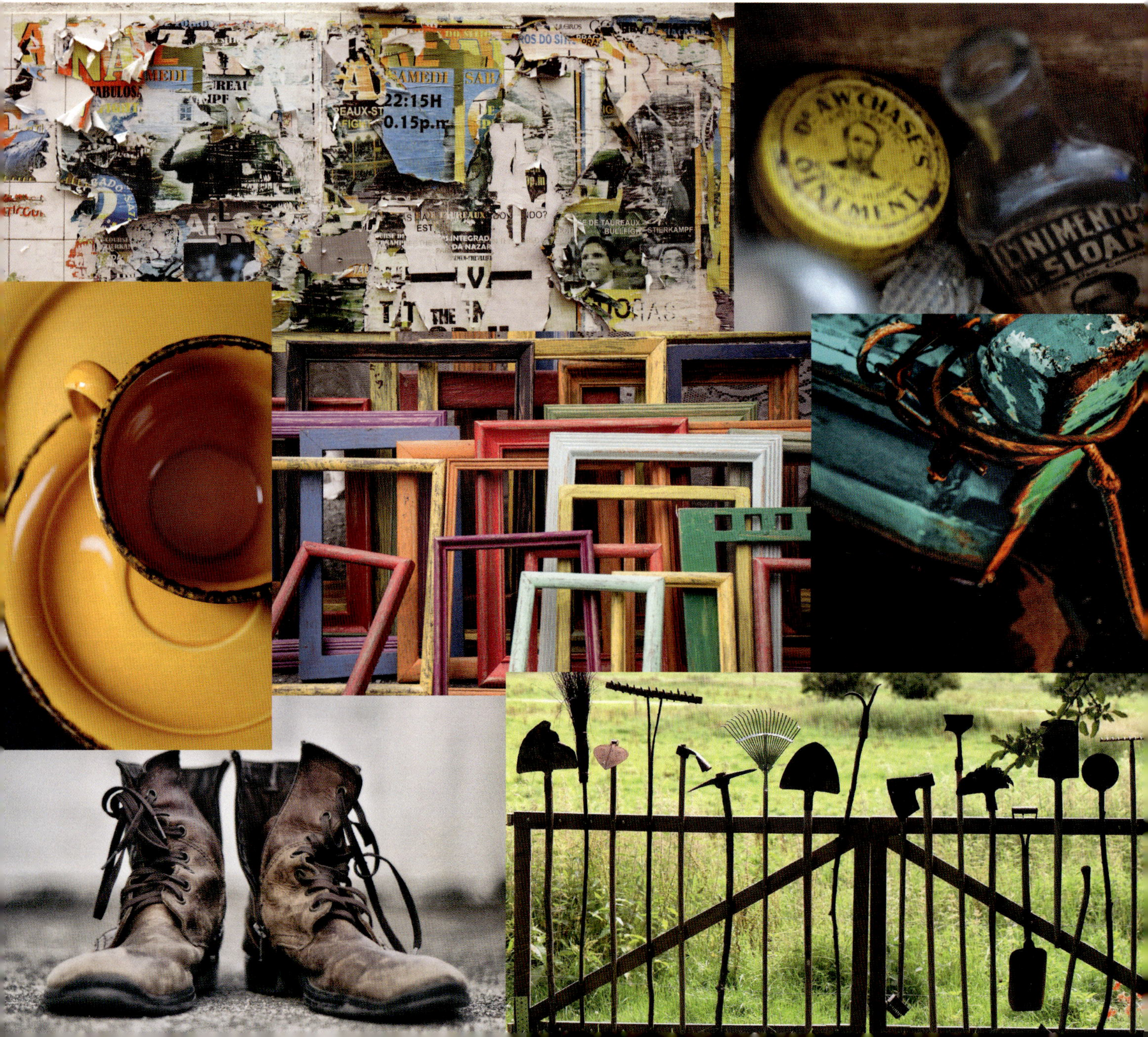

PS. Your underwear does not have to match

Your mother probably told you at least once as a child to make sure if you were going to be run over that you should have your best underwear on. As a lady this generally means your bra and pants should match in polite society. Now I'm telling you to break the rules and live on the wild side, they don't have to match, ever, not even if you plan on getting run over today! I really don't think the doctors are going to mind if your bra is pink and your pants are green or if one sock has stirps and the other has spots, so go wild and mix and match.

The real issue here is that nothing has to match and there are two reasons why.

1. You have the right to be who you want, crinkles, scars, imperfections and everything else, all day every day
2. There are much more important things to do in life than spend time matching your underwear

By embracing your inner Wabi Sabi you will become more grateful for what you have as you learn to love it more. You will be happy using what you already have rather than feeling the need to go out and buy more all the time making you more content and comfortable in your surroundings. You will learn to just 'be', enjoy the simple pleasures and making time to bring more of these into your life.

You will also learn to love yourself more as you grow older and wiser with your belongings, enjoying each moment you spend together. Wabi Sabi gives a way of life that reconnects with what is really you and a chance to be peaceful and at harmony with life giving yourself permission to be exactly who you need to be.

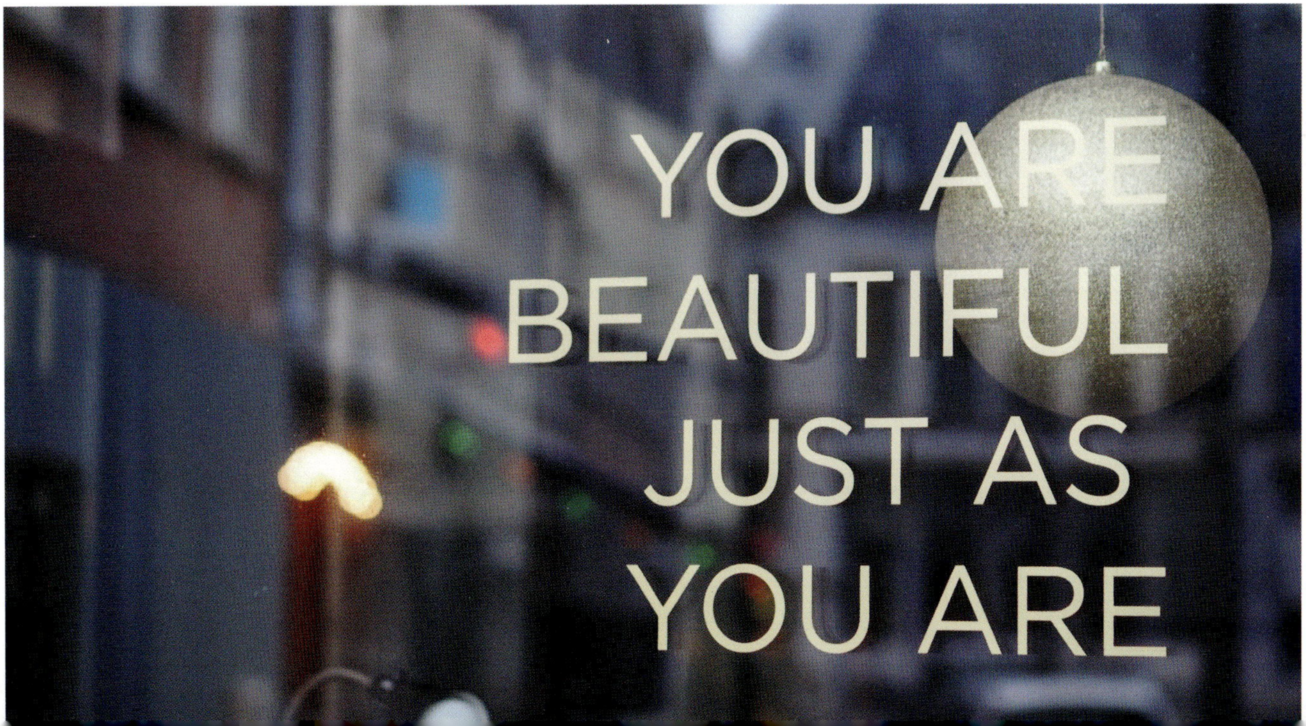

Some ideas for reading and where research for the separate definitions of Wabi and Sabi came from.

- "The Classic Tradition In Japanese Architecture: Modern Versions Of The Sukiya Style", Teiji Itoh, Yukio Futagawa

- "Wabi-Sabi for Artists, Designers, Poets and Philosophers", Leonard Koren

- "Reflections of the Spirit: Japanese Gardens in America", Maggie Oster

And to finish, may favourite thing in the world, you do not get much more Wabi Sabi than Rust.

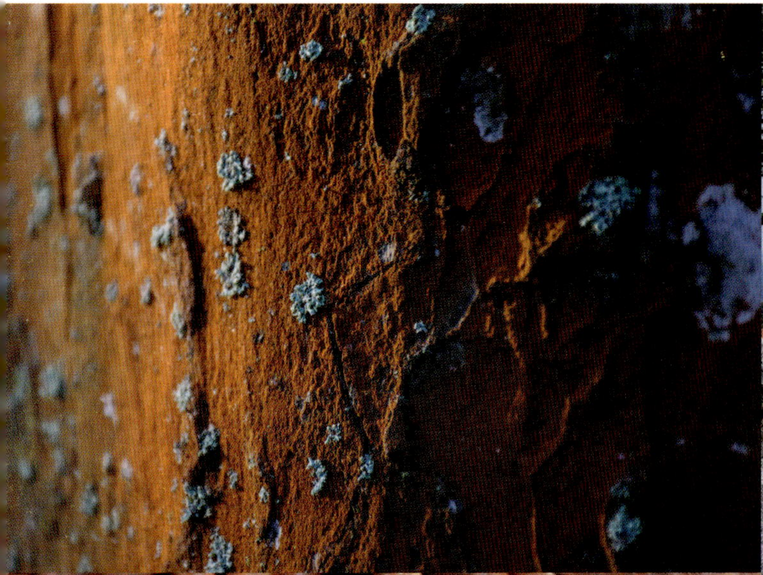

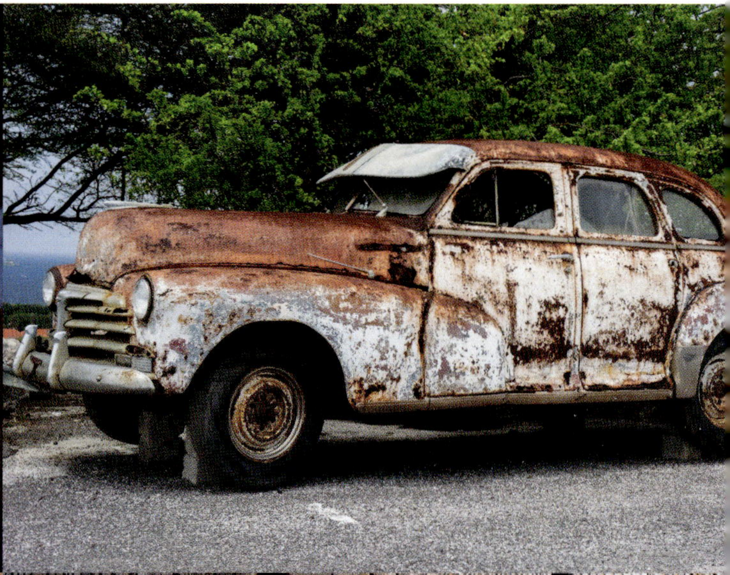

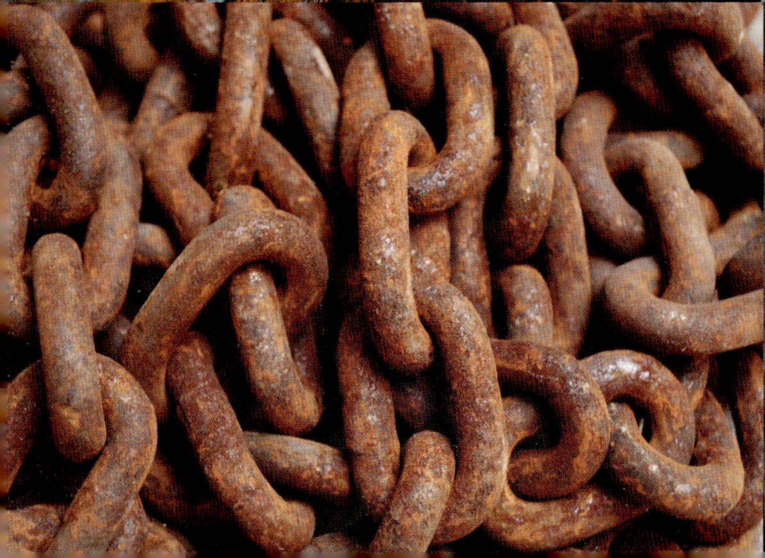

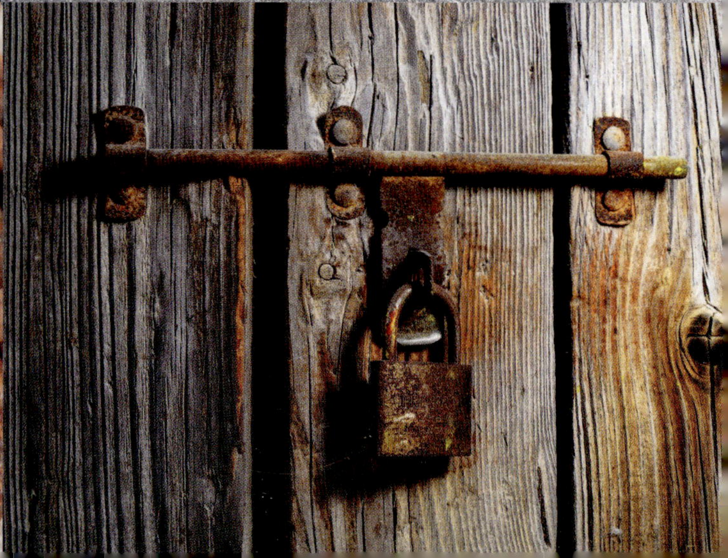